After a Funeral

DIANA ATHILL

GRANTA

Granta Publications, 12 Addison Avenue, London W11 4QR

First published in Great Britain by Jonathan Cape 1986
Paperback edition published by Granta Books 2000
This edition published by Granta Books 2012

A CIP catalogue record for this book is available from the British Library.

1 3 5 7 9 10 8 6 4 2

ISBN 978 1 84708 633 4

Printed and bound by CPI Group (UK) Ltd, Croydon, CR0 4YY

Contents

1 Beginning and End

One evening in the summer of 1963 I ran downstairs to answer the door with special pleasure. The dinner party was supposed to be for an American couple passing through London, but privately I was looking forward to it because of someone else: a man whom I had never met. He had turned up unexpectedly, and when he telephoned I thought 'Lucky I'm giving a party – it's something I can ask him to naturally, without seeming to make too much of our first meeting.'

I wanted to meet him because I loved a book he had written. I had seen in it that when he was funny, as he often was, it was not because he was trying to entertain but because he himself was enchanted by the comedy in the incident he was describing. Getting this incident, these people, this quirk of human behaviour down, and getting it down right – that was what he had been enjoying, rather than 'expressing himself'; and while books written in this way are not necessarily great books, this is the way the great books I love best are written. It is the real thing.

We had exchanged a good many letters about his writing, and I had heard something about him from other people. He was an Egyptian whose passport had been withdrawn because he was a Communist, and he had been living for some years as an exile in Germany. He hated that country. He was very poor, supporting himself by working in factories and docks. From his book it was possible to deduce what his early youth had been like, and to see that this hard exile's life was a dramatic reversal of his circumstances. A German acquaintance had described him as 'a modest, tender and gazelle-like being', which went with the personality suggested by his writing. I was a sucker for oppressed foreigners, and an oppressed foreigner who was a gazelle-like being and who could shrug off hardship in order to look at things with the humour and perceptiveness shown in his book was one whom I would certainly like. He would be more than an interesting new acquaintance. He would be a friend.

When I opened the front door I was, for a moment, disappointed. He looked more like a goat than a gazelle: arched eyebrows, long nose, long upper lip, small neat beard but no moustache – a sardonic face. And he was stiff, a small man in a trim and conservatively cut blue suit with a fraction of white handkerchief at the breast pocket, white shirt, dark tie, answering my greeting with formality from behind a bunch of carnations wrapped in tissue paper. Perhaps he didn't click his heels and bow, but it would not have been surprising if he had done so – and I had come downstairs with both hands out, so to speak, ready to cry 'Hurrah! We're meeting at last!'

I recognized that I had gone further in anticipation of friendship than he had because I knew more about him than he knew about me – I had read his book. As we went upstairs I thought that he would soon relax.

He was gravely courteous on being introduced to my other guests, and then silent, choosing to stand or sit on the edge of the group; the size of the room didn't allow him a position outside it, but that was what he would have preferred. He was watching and listening. If a cigarette needed lighting or a glass had to be disposed of he was quick to notice and to act. His movements were calm and economical: a deft, graceful man, not a bumper or a stumbler. Might he be bored? He was clearly not much interested in the kind of small talk which goes on at the beginning of a party, but he was interested in observing the talkers. His attentive brown eyes made the smallness of the small talk more apparent.

Soon after we had sat down to the meal someone said something more interesting, which related directly to the speaker's experience, and instantly the sardonic goat-face changed. The eyes actually appeared to light up, melancholy gave way to animation. He began to describe something which chimed with what had been said, and he was funny. Everyone laughed. People began asking him about Germany and someone expressed admiration of a Jewish friend who now went back there on business trips. 'He wouldn't do that if he could get into an Egyptian skin from time to time,' he said, and told us how often, when he was in a German bar among strangers, someone would mark the discovery that he was an Egyptian with a look of complicity or a nudge, and would say: 'Ah, *you* will understand, then, that Hitler knew what he was doing.' He was good on Germany, apparently well-informed on politics and trends in public opinion, emphatic on how he disliked the country but fair about its achievements.

When he was questioned about his life as an exile he dodged sympathy by being matter-of-fact, or amusing, or sometimes impatient. The part of this experience he was willing to use in talk was made up of comic predicaments and ingenious devices for survival. When, harking back to his book, I asked about Egypt, he became even more entertaining because the impulse moving him was so obviously one of pleasure. He described things because he was amused or outraged by them, his audience was of secondary importance – he was doing in conversation what he did in writing.

Halfway through dinner I noticed that he didn't like one of his fellow-guests, a pretty woman who had published two novels. I had expected him to enjoy meeting a writer, considering how far he had to live, usually, from people who shared his concerns, but it wasn't working. She was a clever woman, but self-conscious, seeing herself as one who practised an art and had difficulty reconciling its demands with those made on her by ordinary life. Sometimes I had felt that she became rather pompous, almost absurd, in this attitude, but this evening it wasn't showing much. She did, however, contradict the Egyptian quite sharply once or twice about Germany, with which she felt an affinity, and I suspected that she was not enjoying the way he was becoming the centre of attention. He was being elaborately polite to her, with an underlying irony which came at times uncomfortably near the surface.

After dinner he helped me take things into the kitchen, and stacked dishes while I made coffee. My hunch had been right: he was already behaving as an old friend would have done.

'You're being a bit naughty,' I said. 'What have you got against that poor woman? Do leave her alone — she's very nice really.'

'I'm sure she is,' he said, 'but I can't bear that kind of thing — that "being a writer", that taking one's "art" so seriously and all.'

'But you're a writer and you take it seriously.'

'*I am not a writer.*' He sounded quite fierce.

'What do you mean? You are — and a very good one.'

'If I thought I was trying to "make literature", to "write beautifully", I'd never write another word.'

I remembered our correspondence about his book, and how he had always known exactly what he wanted and why he wanted it that way. He was ready enough to accept suggestions which arose from the fact that English was not his first language, but if an alteration changed a nuance of meaning by a hair's breadth, he was intransigent. Every sentence of his seemingly casual prose had been weighed and worked over — he was as careful in his craft as ever this woman had been.

But I knew what he meant. 'She *does* rather carry a sacred flame about,' I said, and we both started to giggle.

'Don't worry,' he said. 'I'll go and sit on the other side of the room by that sweet fat man. I really like him.'

Two of the people who were there that evening asked him to visit them. They were somewhat taken by his exoticness: here was a man to whom things had happened which would never happen to them, things that commanded interest and sympathy. But it was the way in which he took it that charmed his new friends: the humour, the ironic understatement, the lack of self-pity, the undiminished relish for life. 'I don't think I've ever met a more *elegant* man,' my lover said to me one day, and that was indeed the impression he made: someone in whom a sense of style came from the centre and was nearer to being a moral quality than an adornment.

I felt elated when I went to bed that night. One can make plenty of new acquaintances in middle-age, but it is not often that one sees the possibility of knitting a new person into one's life as one did in youth, and that had just happened.

Five years later this man killed himself in my flat. He swallowed twenty-six sleeping pills, and then telephoned a friend. The two most common reactions to this are (from the loving) horror at the thought of his last-minute panic, and (from the knowing) the conclusion that he didn't really mean to die. I believe both these reactions are mistaken. From the message he left me, and from what the friend he called has said about the way he spoke, I think he was needing a witness. It is bad enough merely to collapse in grief when alone; other people's ignorance of what is happening soon makes the tears seem foolish. How much worse to be performing what he called 'the one authentic act of my life' in a vacuum. 'A terrible let-down': he used those words in his last note. Terrible indeed, to be doing something so important as dying by one's own decision without anyone's knowing. He picked up the telephone to make the act real. He himself would feel, I believe, that in writing his book and in choosing his death he did the only two things in his life which belonged to the man he could appear to be, and whom he might, in different circumstances, really have been.

5

2 An Exile

I have described our first meeting, and now I am going to describe how he appeared after I had known him for two years. I can do this without using hindsight, because at the end of that two years I felt the need to sum him up for myself, and therefore wrote a 'portrait' of him. The rest of this chapter is the 'portrait'.

I shall call him Didi. It is inappropriate, but so is the nickname his family uses. There are places where a particular style is preserved long after it has vanished elsewhere – the sediment, usually, left by a receding empire, little pockets of the Austro-Hungarian empire in Eastern Europe, or of the Ottoman empire in Greece. Egypt, or rather his class within it, seems to me such a pocket. It preserves certain features of Edwardian England, and one of these is the nicknames: Dodo, Fido, Fifi, Pussy. And he says that they still play croquet on the lawns of the Gezira Sporting Club.

I have never been in Egypt and have met only a few of his relations. Of his family I know only what he and they have told me, or what I have guessed; but perhaps when nostalgia causes a man to make a legend of his family, what he makes of it will tell something?

They are landowners, and are therefore out of favour with Nasser's regime. The property from which they made their large fortunes has now been taken away from them – or is supposed to have been taken away. There is a big difference between an uncle still close to the land, living in upper Egypt, and those who live in Cairo and Alexandria. When I talked of going to Egypt and wanting to visit some member of the family, Didi said 'Ha! The aunts wouldn't let you see *him*. They'd be very very careful who they let you meet.' Their situation has become precarious, but *on se débrouille*, and surprisingly successfully, or so it seems to an outsider. An aunt of Didi's, discussing shopping in Rome: 'My dear, one can't any more, the prices are terrible. It's impossible to find anything wearable under £150.'*

There are doctors, lawyers and professors in the family, and almost always they are presented as in some way remarkable. 'My mother and her sisters were very beautiful and witty' – 'My father was the best doctor in Egypt' – 'Uncle so-and-so was an alcoholic from when he was seventeen' – 'Uncle such-and-such was the wittiest man in the world but he was mad, he shot himself.' In explanation of the last, from a cousin of Didi's: 'You see we had one ancestor who was syphilitic, so we are often mad.' If Didi is remembering charm, wit, elegance or intelligence he does so with a slightly elegiac gravity; horrors he recalls with sparkle and relish.

His maternal grandparents are important, never spoken of without a glow of pleasure and love in his eyes. They represent wisdom, virtue and benevolence of a kind native to the country. They had a big house, always full of uncles and aunts and cousins, where Didi spent his early childhood, and 'the only duty of everyone was to be happy and laugh. We laughed so much in that house ...'

They also vomited. 'It was a speciality in our family, when we were in love it was physical, we vomited. Everyone was always in love in my grandparents' house – all those cousins – so there was always someone vomiting. When I was six I was in love with my cousin Kiki – she was eight years older than me but it was real love – and one day when I thought I was alone in the garden I did a sad little vomit and she saw me. "So you really do love me!" she said.'

* £150 then was the equivalent of about £700 now.

It is a family which expresses its feelings violently in other ways, too. 'Terrible rows' are frequent. A strong feeling is justified by its strength. When I first met Didi I was impressed by his self-control and the stoic way he bore the depressing hardships of exile in Germany, but I learnt gradually that his control is a balancing trick. He admires self-control but in fact he often abandons himself to the force of gravity with defiant relief.

The family believes itself to have a tremendous generosity of emotion. The two I know best besides Didi are mother and son, Dolly and Mémé. Mémé was in England as a student and his mother came to spend a summer with him because it 'killed' her to be without him, although he went home for the holidays. She took a furnished flat and Didi came from Germany to join them for a few weeks: an island in his exile, which had already lasted for about five years. 'Love' must have been one of the most-used words in that flat. Whether they were talking to each other or about each other, they all constantly declared their love.

That was when I first met Didi, but I had of course corresponded with him over his book. The first time I telephoned him at Dolly's flat she answered in her pretty, husky French accent and was instantly welcoming. 'Please, you must come to us soon, I will cook you an Egyptian meal. You must stay the weekend, we love any friend of Didi's.'

So I went there one weekend for lunch, and from the way Dolly took my hands in both of hers I knew at once that we would kiss when we parted. She had cooked an elaborate and exquisite meal and her mastery surprised me because at home she must have had servants, however reduced her fortune.

'Does your aunt cook when she's at home?' I asked Didi when she was out of the room.

'Good God, no, I don't think she ever goes into the kitchen.'

I asked her when she came back how she did it. 'It's *atavistique*, my dear, *atavistique*. My mother – you remember, *habibi*? – kept such a wonderful table, she always knew exactly how everything should be done. It is only a question of knowing how it should be.'

She was charming, with her slightly haggard face, her

8

well-cut hair and pretty figure, wearing a tweed skirt and cash-mere jersey which exactly matched. And she had a way of light-ing up at the mention of a name: 'I *adore* her – so much charm, such a wonderful nature!' I recognized this manner. I have seen it in Englishwomen of good family and much money. It doesn't preclude shrewd assessments or spiteful judgments; it is a matter of 'good taste', perhaps stemming from the same period as the nicknames. What it chiefly means is 'we can afford to be as gracious and charming in our reactions to people as we are in everything else'. It is a scattering of largesse.

Gracious and charming Dolly certainly was. There was nothing to say but 'I love your aunt'. And her hospitality went beyond the gushing manner. She would share her bedroom, or even her bed, so that Mémé and Didi could have friends to stay, and it was impossible to get near the washing-up. Her image of herself as generous and loving was not without reality, although as I learnt later there were times when she could lapse from the ideal it expressed.

Many of her English friends were grand. She truly believed that she loved them because of how kind, how good, how witty, how generous they were; but these qualities would have been celebrated more perfunctorily if they had been less rich and well-bred. She enjoyed their grandness in itself, and par-ticularly it comforted her. That was how people ought to be, and they were still her friends even in these terrible days when 'it is impossible, you know, we have nothing left. We can't get a penny out of the *fellaheen* any more.' That last remark slipped out when she was entertaining people of her own sort to drinks. She looked round guiltily to confirm that neither her son nor her nephew had heard, knowing that they would have been dis-gusted by it.

Dolly spoke English fluently, but French was more natural to her. All the women of the family were educated at French *pen-sionnats*, all the men at English schools. They broke into Arabic sometimes for family jokes or squabbles, but they told me they spoke it badly.

There were passages of Arabic when we were planning to cheat the insurance company. Didi owned a small and ancient

Volkswagen. Soon after he arrived someone ran into it and it had to be repaired, a matter of three weeks' work. Fortunately the insurance was paid up, so it was not too bad a disaster – indeed, it might be a windfall. They were short of money. Didi had scraped together the bare minimum for his trip, and whatever Dolly had managed to bring out of Egypt (the export of currency was narrowly restricted), she was overspending it recklessly – they made tragi-comedy of their financial plight almost as often as they spoke of love. It didn't take them a moment to see the next move.

Didi *needed* a car, the accident would force him to hire one, and for this the insurance company would have to pay. So where was a friend owning a car who would be prepared to say that he had hired it to Didi and would give him a receipt to show the company for ... how much? £30? Nonsense, for three weeks it would be more than that, what about £50? Yes, but what was the rate for car-hire nowadays? It wouldn't do to claim a sum which looked improbable. 'You see, if Didi really *did* hire a car, the insurance *would* have to pay,' explained Dolly in parentheses, suddenly nervous of my Englishness. Which was true, or the company would not so calmly have accepted as genuine the receipt which I composed and typed out.

I liked the part of Dolly which could so immediately appreciate this scheme: 'saltiness', it is called in Egypt, the tough, sly quality of the underdog rejoicing in scoring off the top dog, so bred into the bones of a colonized people that a streak of it persists even in that people's aristocracy. It can hardly be called a virtue (except that it contributes to endurance), but it is amusing and I found it sympathetic; that, and the conviction with which she believed in any emotion which she might be expressing. She couldn't be disliked, and this remained true even after I had become shocked by the way in which her generous protestations of love could be let down by her actions.

When she returned to Egypt Didi went to the station to see her off, and came to my flat afterwards, shaken. I could see at once that something had gone wrong, but it was some time before I could get it out of him. Then it emerged that Dolly had promised to leave some money with him, knowing that he had none left, not even his fare back to Germany, but at the very last moment, on the platform, had told him that she had spent it all. If he hadn't been counting on it he wouldn't be, as he was now, flat broke. What was he going to do, and how could she, after all her loving talk, have put him in this pickle? There had been a 'terrible scene' – and as he described the recriminations and tears and wailings of 'Now you won't love me any more' which had gone on, Didi, for all his dejection, began to laugh.

'Dolly's love!' he said. 'But the funny thing is, you know, she *does* love me.'

I believed him. She was not the sort of person who could believe in no longer having money . . . and there was something else (acknowledged or unacknowledged?): she knew that Didi wasn't really stranded because I would come to his rescue. After all, *I* hadn't been deprived of my birthright; I must be earning plenty of money in my job; I 'loved' the boy; it wouldn't hurt me.

Before her marriage Dolly brought Didi up. 'I had him from when he was a tiny baby, he is like a son to me.' She looked after him because his mother, her younger sister, wouldn't. His mother was the beautiful one of the family – they all three told me that – and was married in her teens to a man much older than herself, whom, they said, she didn't love. She was too young to want a child, and to make matters worse her husband died soon after Didi was born. 'My mother didn't have much time for me,' he said. He speaks warmly of his childhood with Dolly in his grandparents' house; he likes to draw an idyllic picture of his childhood and tell how he was his grandmother's favourite and how she always kept him at her side, laughing over grown-up gossip with him even when he was little more than a baby. He likes to tell how beautiful and gay Dolly and his mother – he always includes his mother in this – were when they came to kiss him goodnight before going out to a party. But Mémé told me: 'His mother was *horrible* to him, you know, but the funny thing is he adored her, he still does.' Didi himself denied this: 'I enjoy being with her – or I did when I last saw her which was years ago – because she's very charming and amusing, I like her as a woman. But I don't love her.' I have noticed, however, that he always goes out of his way to let me know if any of his few clothes – a cheap shirt or two, and some pyjamas – have been sent by her as a present, and he has told me repeatedly that she gave him the most precious of all his possessions, his little car.

It was not he, but Mémé, who told me the following story. 'When Didi was about eight or ten he came back from school one evening and there was no one at home – ' he had left his grandparents' house for his mother's when she remarried. 'He rang and rang, and no one answered. So he went away and walked round looking at shops and things, and then he came back and rang again, and still no one was there. So he went away, and came back, and went away, and came back, and it wasn't until about eleven o'clock that a servant from the flat above came down and said "Oh there you are, your mother and her husband have gone away for a week. They asked me to tell you and give you this." And he gave him one piastre – *one* piastre – so he could find a telephone and ask someone for a place to sleep. She was always doing things like that. When he won a prize at school and she'd promised to come to the prize-giving, she didn't, and when he cried and asked her why she hadn't come, all she said was why wouldn't he stop being such a nuisance.'

No one could know Didi at all well without understanding that his capacity for loving is deep and candid, and no one could be in a room with him for fifteen minutes without realizing that his pride is supersensitive. His mother was unable to accept his love, or to return it fully, and the rest of the family trampled on his pride. Most of them were rich – some of them very rich – but Didi was a poor relation. 'He was always poor,' said Mémé, 'and my family is so horrible. They talk so much about loving people, but if there was a party, say, and all the cousins were coming, they wouldn't ask Didi. They'd say "Well, he hasn't the right clothes, it would *embarrass* him." And they got all his money, you know – all the money he had from his father. They made lawsuits and got it all.'

'What was he like when he was a child?' I asked.

'I was much younger than him, of course,' said Mémé, 'so I didn't know him properly in those days, but what I can remember about him when he was a boy is that he was always very angry, and shouting.'

That boy is now rarely glimpsed in Didi. He has a strong sense of what he calls 'aristocracy', by which he means the essentials of good-breeding whether inherited or 'natural', and against all the odds he makes an art of elegance. It is easy for him to look well dressed. He owns two suits, one dark blue, one grey with a subdued check, both conservative in cut. Once he told me that his mother sent them to him, and another time that he had bought them in Germany when he received his advance from his book (the truth, I suspect). He preserves these suits with meticulous care and always wears them with a white shirt and a dark tie of knitted silk. He also owns one pair of slacks with worn-out pockets and two or three pullovers. He had no top-coat until I sent him a cheap duffle for Christmas. Whether he is dressed up in one of his suits or not, he manages to look right. His gestures and bearing are naturally elegant, and his manners go with his appearance: a grave, formal courtesy, sometimes a shade elaborate but exceptionally winning, or a natural and responsive gaiety. It is as though he wanted to prove himself more 'the real thing' than any of 'them', however little money or status in the family he has; that he rather than 'they' preserves the essence of his beloved grandparents.

Many Egyptians of Didi's background think wistfully of living abroad but stay at home because if they left they would lose their passports, and they can take no money out. They resent the regime because they are to its right. Didi is forced to live abroad because he is to its left. He was in opposition first (like all his contemporaries) to the British, the foreign people he most loves and admires; then to the Revolution because it didn't go far enough. And had neither of these two things existed to oppose, he would have found something else: the impulse to take a stand against authority was bred, surely, by his family.

Although none of them apart from Dolly gave him love, and although they humiliated him, they did for him what they considered proper. They sent him to a 'good' school and later to a university and abroad, to study medicine. A 'good' school meant an English-type school run by an English headmaster, but perhaps an Egyptian English school is not so English as Egyptians suppose.

'I shall never forget', said Didi, 'the first day X came to school. He was very big, much older than the rest of us, a real peasant. He could hardly speak any English then, and he looked so strange among all those other little boys. And halfway through the morning he suddenly said "Well, it feels to me like time for lunch," and he opened his satchel and brought out a little stove, and a bottle of oil, and a lemon, and garlic, and *foul* [black beans], and calmly began to cook his lunch. All the boys stared at him. He looked round and saw me sitting to one side – I was always sitting rather to one side – watching him [he still sits to one side and watches]. So he said "Hey, you! You look all right. Why don't you come over here." And after that we always did everything together. He was wonderful. You know how I always say what I love best about Egypt is the jokes? Well, making marvellously witty jokes was as natural to X as breathing.'

It may have been this friend who first made Didi feel that his family were not properly 'Egyptians', and that he wanted to identify with the 'proper Egyptians' against them, which landed him with the poor and the oppressed. His political awareness, nourished by avid if haphazard reading, soon went beyond the nationalistic sport of 'Away with the British!'

When the Revolution came he was happy because it would sweep away what his family represented, but its sweeping was far from thorough and then, in its turn, it began to oppress. It oppressed Jews and it oppressed Communists. Didi began to be drawn to Jewish girls, and he became a Communist.

This, of course, is oversimplification. He also had good rational grounds for criticizing the Revolution. The Arab-Israel conflict *is* likely to be ruinous to the Middle East, so that in writing schoolboyish articles attacking Nasser for cherishing that conflict and spending the country's resources on building up an army for it, Didi was talking sense. That, it seems, was the immediate cause of his exile. He doesn't only imagine that he feels passionately about these things: his intelligence and the generosity of his nature are genuinely outraged by them. But his intelligence also tells him that Nasser has much to his credit. When I said to him 'If you really care so passionately about the *fellaheen* it would have made more sense to keep quiet and get on with doing what you could on the side of the good in the Revolution,' he answered sadly 'Do you think I haven't told myself that a thousand times?'

Didi has clear sight, but it often fails to govern his actions. Indeed it is often a burden to him because it makes him able to judge the actions which spring from factors beyond his control. He knows that a position of impotence as an exile in Germany is no place from which to champion the *fellaheen* – but there he is, stuck in Germany for so long as he can foresee. He knows that if he had completed his medical training he would be a more useful man and a more secure one, but he threw it over. He told me once that he did this because he wanted to write, but it was not convincing. He avoids speaking plainly about it. Was it just that 'they' wanted him to be a doctor, or did he get into some kind of trouble of which he is too ashamed to speak? He might well have wrecked his prospects by some folly because he has a strong impulse towards self-destruction.

Didi is a gambler ('Of course!' I thought when I learnt this, though I had seen little of him then). He does without it almost all the time, of necessity, not counting poker or belotte with friends. These are games; gambling is different – serious. If he suddenly received a lot of money I think he would first summon up his precise, orderly, 'sensible' side and allot so much of it to paying off his debts, so much to buying things he lacked, and then he would make for a casino. If the sum were too small to make an impression on his debts he would skip the first stage. When he last found a job after a long and hard period without one he ate and drank and smoked his first month's pay, but used the next instalment for gambling and lost the lot. Whether he wins or loses is irrelevant, or rather his pleasure in the first or annoyance at the last is disconnected from his sensations about gambling in itself: it is the act which draws him.

'Of course we aren't going to play, how can we? We'll just go in and have a look.' He said that once to Mémé and me, but as Mémé noticed, 'He wasn't listening to anything we said, his eyes went glassy.' We couldn't play because we had no money beyond that for our hotel. I told myself that as Didi had recognized this we would be all right, but his eyes *had* gone glassy, and it soon became evident that he was capable of lying to get through that door, and that if we dragged him away he would sneak out and return after we had gone to bed.

I watched him at the table. It was a matter of ritual for him to appear relaxed. His face was impassive, his stance carefully nonchalant, one hand in pocket; he placed his chips as though casually and while the wheel was spinning he turned away and looked out over the room. He was seeing nothing. He had withdrawn and gone still. I soon left him, feeling that the presence of someone to whom affection and politeness obliged him to pay attention was an irritation. I only saw him losing, but no doubt he would have won with exactly the same show of indifference.

That time he left the table at a point where he had broken even, drawn away from it not by commonsense but by kindness: Mémé, who was too young to be admitted, was waiting sadly outside. If Mémé had not been there he could, I felt sure, have lost his hotel money quite cheerfully and landed us in a pretty pickle. I have never known him gamble at any other time without losing everything he had on him.

He also drinks too much. He fancies himself as a civilized drinker and insists that he is safe from alcoholism because of this. It is true that he likes to decide carefully on the place, the company, the liquor, and that once the decision is made he will approach the occasion with ceremony; but when he has started he doesn't stop until money, drink, the party or his capacity (which is large) comes to an end. And besides this greediness when he is drinking for pleasure, he will drink anything he can lay hands on, even if he has to steal it, when suffering becomes too much for him.

Since his Egyptian passport was withdrawn, Didi has often been penniless. Unable to get a permit to work in England, where he wanted to live, he had to make his way in Germany, without at first knowing the language and without any qualifications for earning a living. He has worked in the Hamburg docks, as a labourer, in factories and as a clerk. He is good at figures and with his hands – broad peasant hands which look incongruous because the rest of him is finely made. He can be methodical and orderly and he has never complained of the kind of work he has had to do. When people are sorry for him he becomes almost cross. Although he has never said so, he may feel that these are the kinds of job a Communist ought to do; or, on the other hand, a way of life so remote from the one his background makes natural to him may seem less humiliating, because more dramatic, than one only a few rungs down the ladder. Anyway, he makes no fuss about doing humble work, turns up in the morning even if still drunk, and although he has left jobs and has lost them through illness, being sacked doesn't figure in his stories.

There have been spells when he could find no work, was thrown out of rooms and came near to starving. The winter he finished his novel he lived in an unheated cellar – unheated until he discovered a way of leading a wire from the next-door house's electricity supply into his room. I have seen a photograph of the heater he improvised, of which he was proud: a spidery coil of wire between two structures of brick. After he had sold his book he rang at the neighbours' door, told them what he had done, and offered to pay – and they called the police. 'It's funny, but the police in Germany are impeccable, they have always been very nice to me. It's the ordinary people I loathe.' Some of the ordinary people, however, have been uncommonly good to him. Once he sat on a bench in a square thinking 'I suppose I shall have to kill myself, it would be better than dying of cold and starvation,' only to be saved by a man he scarcely knew. He had been living in an attic above a pub and this man came to the bar often and sometimes bought Didi a drink because he enjoyed talking about foreign parts. 'Where's the young Egyptian?' he had asked, and the publican said that he had thrown him out. The man got into his car and drove round the town until he found Didi on his bench, and took him home, and kept him there for three months. It was a small house – Didi had to share a bedroom with two little girls – and they were poor, though the man's business prospered later. It was this incident which rooted Didi in that particular town.

In spite of taking a purring pleasure in any luxury which comes his way, Didi never complains of the often very austere conditions in which he has had to live. What he does complain of, and bitterly, is the loneliness. During five years in Germany he has met people who are kind and pleasant – he has quite a large circle of drinking, card-playing friends in the town where he settled – but he has met hardly anyone with whom he can talk. This makes him homesick for London more than for Egypt, because it was in London, when he was here as a student, that he first escaped from his background into a carefree and bohemian freedom which he has romanticized ever since.

Another suffering of exile is having to be grateful. Didi is disaster-prone, and other people besides the man in the pub have had to pick up the pieces, and have done it cheerfully because of the attraction of his personality; he has often had no alternative to accepting kindness. He loves kindness – he glows when he speaks of it – but he suffers from 'appalling gratitude pains'. They make him want to 'become very small, shrink up to nothing and be invisible'. In these moods the word 'little' will start occurring often in his letters: 'back in my little room' – 'safe in my little car' – 'sitting in a corner like a little mouse'. This mouselike mood clamped down on his pride usually bodes ill.

I have only seen one brief appearance of the boy 'who was always very angry, and shouting', but I know of others from his letters. The one I saw took place when he decided pessimistically that the insurance company we were cheating was not, after all, going to pay up. Five days had passed without an answer from them, and he began to rage against 'these crooks'.

Did I know a good lawyer, he was not going to be treated like this by these crooks. I pointed out that these things always take time, and that anyway very little time had passed: write again, I suggested, or perhaps go to see them? Dolly backed me up, and suddenly Didi was striding about the room and shouting 'How can I visit them? I can't deal with these bloody crooks!' He was trembling, and yelling at the top of his voice.

Dolly yelled back 'Don't shout at me like that!' and he crashed out of the room, some kind of panic in his sudden fury. Fifteen minutes later he returned, calm, and admitted that we were right. While the scene was going on I had been amazed and rather disgusted at his childishness, but on his return I felt a curious kind of concern and admiration, as though in mastering his nervous rage he had mastered something more threatening than it appeared to be. It did not seem surprising when this incident was followed by a typical disaster: he visited the company, came away with a cheque for the hire of the imaginary car as well as the repairs to the real one – and the next day Dolly called me in tears to tell me that he'd had his wallet, with all the money in it, stolen.

The second time I knew him to 'take off' in this way was over a contract with a German publisher. Its terms were tough, but customary. He could have improved them a little if he had argued, but he had not even read the short and uncomplicated document before signing it, which was not the publisher's fault. When, much later, he discovered what the terms were, he declared that he would rather his novel was never published in Germany than accept them. I told him that he *had* accepted them, and through no one's fault but his own, but he refused to listen, becoming more hysterical as the argument continued. The German publisher agreed to improve the terms a little, but instead of being satisfied Didi became even angrier. He had cast the German publisher, by then, as a blood-sucking capitalist, and wrote as though defending a high moral cause. Realizing that he was embracing the situation with a mad relish, I tried to play it down; but all he answered was 'If you *order* me to accept, I will, but only because I'm fond of you.' Refusing him this ridiculous way out, I repeated that he must accept his own responsibility for the situation, accept the improvement he had been offered, and then, when his next book was written, negotiate a new contract which suited him better.

His reply to this was a letter of triumph. He had cancelled the contract. That bastard had thought he couldn't because it meant repaying £500, but now he knew better, now he knew that he couldn't treat Didi like mud. A friend had produced the money; he would be joint owner with Didi of the rights in his work until the £500 was paid off.

There were few rights left to sell in the existing novel – certainly not £500-worth – and the next book appeared to be far from finished, besides which Didi would need every penny he could make from it. If that generous but foolish friend ever got his money back he would be lucky. And what had Didi gained? He had lost the pleasure of having the book appear in Germany; he had let himself in for the worst 'gratitude pains' yet; all he had gained was a moment of perverse emotional release. When he complained later that the contract need not have been cancelled, saying of the German publisher 'he handled me the wrong way', I could have spanked him.

Didi's self-destructive impulse appears most strongly when he is in love. 'I am always in love. I only stop being in love with one woman when I fall in love with the next.' The cards are stacked against him from the start because of his stubborn belief that people only love intensely if they are not loved in return. Against protests he puts on a smug, knowing look, and quotes cases. 'I could make any woman love me if I had the strength of mind,' he says. All he would have to do, it seems, is to keep up the right kind of indifference at the right time.

He didn't talk like this, however, about the Swedish girl he once wanted to marry. He lost his passport at that time, and how could he ask her to share his stateless existence? His pride, and his romantic idea of what marriage should be, are genuine. But the end of that story as I heard it is so typical of him that it is hard to believe that he himself didn't make it so.

'Her father got fed up at last,' said Mémé. 'He said that either they must marry or it must end. And how could Didi marry her? So he went away to Germany although he loved her very much. But after a bit he got some money – only a very little, but some, from his father's estate. He couldn't bear it any more, so he wrote to her and they arranged to meet in Hamburg and get married there. And on the way there he had a car smash.'

It was a bad smash. Didi was unconscious for days and in hospital for weeks. The girl arrived in Hamburg and he wasn't there. She went back home believing that he had simply chosen not to turn up, and took a job abroad to save her face. When at last he was able to write, the letter took a long time to reach her, and she refused to believe his explanation. Didi says that he was near death in the hospital, and near it again after he was discharged, saved only by an English girl, an old friend, who happened to be teaching in Hamburg and who rescued him. I have met this girl, and what she knew of the story was different. Rescue him she did – he was ill and starving when she found him, and in and out of hospital because of various disasters – but she had the impression that he had been prevented from meeting the Swedish girl only by passport difficulties. 'Which accident?' she asked. 'He had so many! Perhaps he was rolling them all up into one, but I don't know.'

The romantic story as he told it, and as Mémé knew it, sounds too good to be true, but certainly it represents in Didi's mind the ill-fated ending of a genuine love, and certainly it sums up a truth about him: that on the threshold of anything promising he is always frustrated by disaster *apparently* beyond his control.

Since then his loves have been either trivial or unhappy. He is hungry for a great love but gloomily sure that he can never enjoy one since he can see no prospect of being able to get married decently. The trivial affairs he despises, so he turns them into tragedy in an attempt to redeem them: witness what happened with Inge.

Inge moved into a room above his. She was a barmaid, and 'barmaids in Germany', he said, 'aren't like in England, they are usually more or less tarts. She'd slept with pretty well every man in town by then, and naturally she was soon sleeping with

21

me.' A convenient arrangement: only one flight of stairs to go up, and she had a good room with a stove for cooking, where he could be fed and warm of an evening. Soon he was spending most of his time up there, and they had slipped into a domesticated pattern; but Didi would never take her out to meet his friends.

'I am horrible to her,' he told me. 'It makes her very angry, and she's quite right. But I *can't* go out with her, I'm ashamed of her, she's so ... ugly.'

I thought this disgusting, and said so. He agreed with ironical detachment. 'And you see,' he said, 'the funny thing is that because I don't love her and treat her so badly, she fell in love with me. It was bound to happen.'

Inge told him that the situation was becoming unbearable and that it must end. 'She was right, of course, so I stopped going upstairs and she started going out with other men.' No sooner did she start doing that than Didi was in torment. Within a week he was desperate for her, he was in love. She took him back; relief and happiness; and then the same thing all over again. Their relationship became cyclic, one of them on, one of them off, and it went on like that for several months. When Didi first told me about it they were in a period of calm and he claimed that they were cured. 'Now we are just very good friends, thank heavens. She's a very good friend to me — it was she who lent me the money to insure the car.' He laughed as he remembered himself creeping upstairs to put threads of cotton in her door so that he could tell whether she had come in while he was out, and how he had won one round by persuading an ex-girlfriend to stay in his room with him for three days.

During his visit to England he could talk of it as past history, but he had to go back to Germany. He arrived desperate at having glimpsed London again, and his family, for so short a time, and had to endure a gruelling spell without work and was down to living on tea and bread before he found a job as a clerk in the Pay Corps of the British Army. Then he could eat and smoke again, and drink beer on Saturdays, and the work was easy, among Englishmen whom he found amusing, and in an agreeable place. Before two months were up he was writing

'I'm afraid this contentment is bad for me, I am in danger of losing my capacity for despair which is very valuable to me.' I was beginning to know Didi. 'Watch it!' I said to myself, and I was right. Only two letters later the great Inge catastrophe began.

They had resumed their affair and to begin with it had gone smoothly enough to contribute to the dangerous contentment, but on New Year's Eve Didi went to a good party, and he didn't take Inge. She kept quiet, but this time it was conclusive. Two weeks later they were in her room and decided that they wanted some beer. Didi was going for it, but he couldn't find his shoes so Inge went instead. She didn't come back. She met a man in the bar and went off with him.

'I am sorry I haven't written for some time, but I've been having passion-trouble ...' To start with the letters were amused: he was suffering, he said, but how absurd to suffer over 'this bitch' whom he didn't love, didn't even find physically attractive any more. How absurd that he had started to put threads in her door again, to listen for her steps on the stairs ... One paragraph would be a detached description of his ridiculous state, the next a melodramatic account of torment, then back to irony again: 'Luckily there is a streak in me which takes a sort of pleasure in all this.'

At first I paid more attention to the lucidity of the self-analysis than I did to the outcries of misery, expecting that I would soon be hearing of a new girl; but in letter after letter it was still Inge, and gradually the despair began to overcome the lucidity. 'Knowing that it's absurd is all very well, but it doesn't make any difference. I can't eat any more, my throat shuts up, and it's three nights since I've been able to sleep.'

Then there came a frantic letter. Inge had brought a new man to the house. Didi heard them on the stairs, passing his door, then the sounds of their love-making above him. One evening he rushed upstairs after the man had gone, broke the door open and beat Inge up. Other lodgers came running in their dressing-gowns and his landlady pulled him off the girl and was now throwing him out. He was appalled by what he had done, and even more appalled by the violence of his own despair. He was afraid that he might kill himself. He had tried to once, he now said, when he was sixteen, and had been found in time by a happy accident. He had just passed a night so bad that he could imagine slipping into it again, and he was terrified.

After that his letters became drunker and drunker, written at three or four in the morning, either tragic or wildly gay, the smell of the whisky or the cognac on them. 'Don't worry any more, I'm almost over it now. Just finished a bottle of cognac ...' and then an account of a wild time. A swing became evident between despair and elation, with every now and then a short, unnaturally cool note as though he had forced himself to grasp the pendulum and hold it still for a moment.

Finally the friend who had lent him the money to pay off the German publisher intervened and carried him off for a week's skiing. There was intense relief at being physically removed from the situation, exuberant joy at the skiing. 'For the first two days I sang all my favourite songs all the time and I don't think I thought of Inge once.' On the third day he broke his leg.

Soon after that, while his leg was still in plaster, Mémé and I went to meet him for a long weekend in Bruges. We met at nine in the morning after all-night journeys, in the sleazy lounge of the only Belgian address we knew, a hotel in Brussels, where the smell of the morning's coffee mixed with the smell of last night's cigars and became unappetizing. Mémé and I had arrived much earlier and had killed time by walking in a drizzle round the grey sleeping town, our own lack of sleep, and the weather, making us sure that Didi would fail to turn up. When we saw his car outside the hotel we ran to find him in the lounge. The excitement of greeting disguised his appearance, but once the embraces and cries of joy were over we saw that he was very thin, his skin yellow and dull with deep rings of shadow under his eyes. He was ill – evidently as ill as he looked, since he admitted it and he is usually impatient of physical illness and plays it down. He had 'a sort of abscess', hadn't eaten or slept for two days, and had been in pain throughout his long drive. Mémé offered to go out to buy painkillers, but he said 'No, no pills, I can't take any more. It's pills which caused this.' Sleeping pills, pep pills, tranquillizers: it became obvious that he had been living on them, and on drink, for weeks.

So ill did he seem that Mémé and I began to plot getting him back to Germany and into the hands of a doctor, but he wouldn't hear of it: an exact description – 'wouldn't hear' – of Didi refusing something. At first there is a polite, slightly amused but adamant 'no', then at persistence he withdraws, he is not there, not hearing, and the speaker is put into a position of absurd importunity. I saw that if he were to be managed it would have to be done as Dolly would do it: a big scene with screams and tears and emotional blackmail. Against someone unable to mount a scene he was impregnable.

He went to a doctor of his own accord when we reached Bruges, and came back with medicine and a veto on alcohol, and we went to our rooms for a few hours' sleep. I got none for thinking 'My god, what has he done to himself, what will become of him?'

But the medicine worked, the pain went off, and soon he was eating with his usual gusto. Because he could neither walk nor drink we did little for four days but sit about talking, Didi and Mémé enjoying an orgy of family reminiscence which Didi is always capable of turning into entertainment for anyone. Whether it was an idyllic recreation of days on the beach at Alexandria, the dirt on some prosperous uncle, or a drama in which an aunt said to her son 'All right then, go on, shoot yourself,' and he did, falling dead at her feet, he told it with such skill and enjoyment that he could always hold an audience; and Mémé's delighted participation – he had been away from home long enough to share his cousin's nostalgia – made him excel himself. For those four days the feeling between the cousins really was love.

On the fourth day Didi felt enough recovered to announce before lunch that we would go to a pleasant-looking bar and have 'a little aperitif of white wine'. Mémé and I were pleased: a glass or two now could do him no harm, we felt, and would do us much good. It was a small bar, warm on a cold day, no one there but the proprietress and the waitress. Yes, they had a good Moselle, and were pleased to be asked for it in beer-drinking Belgium. It was brought up dusty from the cellar, an ice bucket was found, nuts and cubes of cheese sprinkled with celery salt were provided – Didi somehow made them join in his game of ceremony. It was a delicious wine, and the big fair waitress blushed with pleasure at the charming way he invited her to join us for a glass. 'But first,' he said, 'would you be kind enough to bring us up another bottle.' – 'Another bottle?' she said in surprise, because we had still only tasted the first, and can't have looked a hard-drinking group; a middle-aged woman, a gracefully drooping schoolboy, and a sick-looking man walking with two sticks. I said 'Do we really want another, Didi? This is only an aperitif, after all.'

'We do want another,' he said gently, 'because I am going to drink it myself.' Which he did, and another whole bottle that evening, before we drove over to the casino in Ostende.

When we said goodbye the next day he was again looking yellow and shadowy round the eyes, although he insisted that the illness was over and that it was only grief at seeing us go away. 'Sometimes,' he said, 'I think I should never visit England or see people I love, like this, because it's so terrible when it ends.' He tried to mock at his own lugubriousness, but the loneliness of his exile surrounded him like a cloud as he stood on the quay. The loneliness, and something else. I was not able to define why I felt such a weight of foreboding for him, but I felt it: again 'My god, what has he done to himself, what will become of him?'

Mémé and I comforted each other that in those four days his physical improvement had been evident; that at the casino, whatever recklessness could be sensed in him, he had in fact behaved sensibly; and that the affair with Inge really was over. He had dismissed it as a joke, with hardly the patience to speak of it, and he had told Mémé that he had already found another girl: 'Not serious, he isn't in love or anything, but I think she's going to live with him so he'll be looked after.' (The girl should be pitied, I felt, but who cared about some unknown girl so long as Didi's relish for life and his writing energy could be restored?) He had talked, too, with resigned good sense about living in Germany: 'It's absurd and sentimental to go on pining for England when it won't have me, and anyway I've had more kindness in Germany than I ever had there.' Sensible and calm; nothing in the evidence to cause anxiety. But when he spoke like that his voice and expression became a little hard, and at any moment when he was not responding to talk or laughter, a look of deep, settled melancholy covered his face like a mask. I could tell myself as firmly as possible that there was nothing more than usual to worry about for him, but it was after that meeting that I first asked myself: 'Is he mentally sick?'

The girl he told Mémé about can only have been a stop-gap, because while he never mentioned her to me, he was soon writing about another one, with whom he was not living. 'Why can I never fall in love with simple people? Ursula is complicated, elegant, very sure of herself, older than me. I have got it badly, I am even "courting" and go and play cards with her mother in the evenings.' He was in a state of frenzy but the girl said 'Why must you do everything in a rush? There is plenty of time, I won't fly away,' and he admitted that she was right. The first letters about her, though agitated, were cheerful.

Then came a short one which was a distillation of rapture. She had consented, she had slept with him, it was spring, the leaves, the sun . . . an absurd little letter, but happiness showered out from it like dazzle from a sparkler. 'Let this be it!' I thought. 'Why *shouldn't* poor Didi find a girl who suits him and loves him? He's not too old to break a pattern – let this be it!' But before my answer to his radiant note can have reached him there came another letter, of pure misery. Then another, and another.

They were baffling and they became irritating. They were, simply from the fact of having been written, cries for help, but how could help be given? What had happened? Usually his letters were vivid and concrete like his serious writing, describing incidents and people, relishing absurdities, full of the kind of gossip we both enjoy; but now events, facts and personalities had vanished. It was only his state of mind the letters contained, his despair and hopelessness. It seemed probable that the events behind them were no more than a broken date or the girl's apparent interest in another man at a party, and that he omitted them because he knew their inadequacy as causes of his mood. I felt that his despair had detached itself from any cause and that he was using Ursula as, earlier, he had used Inge: as a point of departure into a state which existed on its own.

One Friday night, thinking about him as I lay in my bath, I said to myself 'Let's face it, I was right, he's a nut.' It was true that his isolation and loneliness made him vulnerable – would make anyone vulnerable – to this kind of suffering, but the letters were not normal. The pendulum swing, the insufficiency of the causes ... I wished I knew more about depressive conditions, because from what little I did know it seemed obvious that a depressive condition was what he was in. The next morning I received a letter from him in which he said 'I am mad'.

It started on a deliberately dramatic note – 'I am writing this early in the morning – very early in the morning' – but as it went on the theatricality fell away. He had just spent a terrible night trying to think out his condition, and he could not escape the conclusion that he was insane. 'Not mentally insane, emotionally insane. This horrible mental sanity which makes me able to see it, and know I can do nothing about it.' It was not a new thing, he said, it had been going on for a long time: fits of despair, hopelessness, disgust with life and disgust with himself. And when he tried to force himself out of it and behave normally it was worse, because every moment of it had to be deliberate (it was something of that, of course, that I had glimpsed in Bruges). 'For the last six days I have not been drinking, not a drop. My behaviour has been so normal and wise, even going for walks and "acting" so sane. Reasonable. Not too much coffee, not too many cigarettes, to bed at eleven, a shower in the morning, washing the car, trying to write, reading, being polite and charming to my visitors. But I have only been doing what my mind tells me to do because although insane I know what sane behaviour is and "act" accordingly' ... 'Only acting, only acting' ... 'To realize it, to see it, and not to be free to do what I should do because of my love for you and Mémé and Dolly' – 'What shall I do?' ... 'I don't know what to do, I don't.'

He returned to his 'lack of freedom' several times. He longed, he said, for an accident so that he could die without knowing how he was hurting the people he loved (each time adding reassurance, to himself as well as me: 'Don't worry, I shan't make an accident happen intentionally.') He ended: 'I shan't even say I'm sorry to write like this because of how hypocritical that would be. All I need do is not send it. But I shall send it, because utter loneliness on top of all this would be even more unbearable.'

Didi had become, it seemed to me, someone in whom loss or frustration could act like a bent wire poked down a drain to recover something, bringing up not only the object but also strings and lumps of horrible deposit which had been hidden there for who knows how long. He had become an inviter of wounds and a potential victim of them because any one of them could re-animate the one inflicted on him when, long before he could defend himself, he was not wanted. He couldn't love if he was loved in return because he could only believe in the fugitive and unloving as a love-object; only know love as the loneliness and pain which he had learnt as a child.

To Didi psychiatrists are a joke: one of those nonsensical American fads. The further East you go, the further back in time in relation to psychiatry, and an incomplete medical training would not do much to alter such an attitude. I knew this, but still I could only tell him, with all the emphasis of concern, that if one knows oneself mentally ill the only course is to consult a specialist. Then I sat back to wait for the next letter, which I expected and feared would be elated. It came almost at once.

Didi's passions in writing are few and profound, because he is impatient of anything but the great. The writers he loves best are Céline and the Russians, particularly Chekhov, whom he reads and rereads with endless joy. ('If at times I say "Why was I ever born?" – I can answer "But to read Chekhov".') What he asks of writing is truth. He distrusts shapelessness, polish, story-making, although verbal virtuosity enchants him (he loves Nabokov). He may sometimes be prevented from seeing the good in some writing because of the presence of qualities he distrusts (though this may be my own resentment speaking, because he doesn't like mine), but he is never taken in by anything phoney and he himself is determined to go beyond artfulness into truth.

Perhaps it is not, therefore, surprising that it was Henry Miller who now called him up from the depths, for even if one thinks that Miller often defeats his own ends by the woolliness of his expression, one can't deny that he has spent his life fighting his way through 'artfulness' to the raw truth. To me he often seems to fail, but to Didi, at that moment, he was sanity.

Long ago, on a superficial reading, he had dismissed *Tropic of Cancer*. Now, having bought a copy to send Mémé, he had looked into it idly, and lightning had struck.

It is one of the most beautiful pieces of literature [when Didi uses that word he uses it carefully and gravely – it is his accolade] I have come across. I think it is going to change my life … It is a revelation – suddenly I saw what a piddle, a piece of pipi, me and my whining and despair. If you read *Tropic* and then come across my novel, or your book, or [half a dozen currently successful writers] they make you or rather me want to vomit. I took that novel I have been writing and stuck it in the toilet and many of my friends and particularly me have used the paper and the words on it for exactly what it should be used for. I am only sorry I did not read *Tropic* before I published the first book, because I'd have stuck that one where I've just stuck this one – a whole novel which would hardly amount in depth, understanding and perception to one simple phrase in *Tropic of Cancer*.

There were seven sides to this letter, which ended 'I didn't send this just after writing it because of fear that it might be just one of my "moments". But no, God be praised. Reading *Tropic* has suddenly made me grow up … I am all right now, and in a feverish haste to write, to write.'

Four days later he was still reporting: 'Reading Miller has put me right back on earth.' He added:

> He too, you see, had something fantastic in him to express and felt the misery of not getting it out easily. I do not regret throwing my manuscript away. Perhaps it was that which was eating me, writing something tepid and mediocre and knowing all the way it was not what I wanted, not what I feel, that my insides want to gush out with something dazzling, some volcano I have to let erupt, and not just another bloody 'novel'. I am in a feverish state of writing, and quite happy.

In all that Didi had told me about his 'despair' his writing had never been mentioned except casually. I told myself I must give him the benefit of the doubt, but I didn't believe that what had been eating him was anything to do with his writing. He had always known, and had very often said, that sincerity and passion were what he valued most in writing, so his 'discovery' in Miller of their vital importance was not a discovery at all. And I knew that feeling – most writers know it – of having 'something dazzling' inside (quickly ... now ... if only one can press the right button something different will happen, something new and far more important ...). It is illusory. It may have something to do with the process of gestation, or be a stage in the collection of creative energy, but what comes out at that time almost always has to be scrapped, and what finally comes out is always another book of the kind you write, never something totally new. Didi was never going to write a 'volcano'; it was not his style.

I concluded sadly – indeed with horror – that his manuscript had been sacrificed unnecessarily: that he had simply used Miller as a launching pad out of despair, as he had used Inge and Ursula as launching pads into it. But would the experience be the less useful for that? Whatever the mechanism which released him from depression, if he had been released, who cared? It was appalling that the book on which he had been working for so long should have been destroyed, but his hold on sanity was more important than his book.

He was released. The following months were hard ones because he was physically ill, unable to work, and penniless, but he was cheerful. Later, however, he was to introduce a puzzling element into his recovery. One day, he told me, he must let me see the account he wrote in his diary of how he emerged from that crisis, because 'it was strange, very strange'. Soon afterwards he sent me the diary, and it was strange, though not in the way he meant.

He sent me a vividly written account of a night he had spent dissuading a desperate girl whom he disliked from killing herself: a tedious, exhausting night, but for him it had a glorious significance. Watching this girl, wearily arguing with her, following her round, drying her tears, mopping up her drunken vomit, listening to her hysterical insults when she turned against him because of what he had said about the man she was despairing over, he had a sudden revelation: this was himself! This pathetic, disgusting, pitiable, boring girl was a mirror in which he was seeing himself. And suddenly he found himself free to reject what he saw; to reject it so completely that he could never be like that again.

It was as though the Henry Miller 'revelation' had never happened. Not only was there no mention of it then or since, but its effects had been wiped out of the story. He might simply have 'rewritten' the last few months of his life, substituting the desperate girl incident for the Henry Miller incident.

I haven't questioned him about this. I would like to understand the tricks he played on himself, but I am scared of blundering. The mechanisms improvised by people in his state to keep themselves going must be vulnerable − patched up of string and safety-pins, so to speak, rather than properly built − and no doubt they could be jolted out of gear in unforeseen ways, so it is better not to touch. What matters is that Didi, although doubly threatened by the wound he carries inside him and the lonely insecurity of exile, *has* managed to haul himself through that crisis and says that he feels happy and strong, and capable of making decisions, and is now writing a thousand words a day.

3 A Guest

That was how I had come to see Didi (I might as well go on calling him that) two years after meeting him. The outlines were to remain unchanged, but there was to be much shuffling of detail and I still had a lot to learn about the complexities of his sickness.

When I wrote that portrait I still believed almost everything Didi told me. Often I was right to do so, because there were times when he was capable of piercing honesty; as both his published writing and his diary proved, he could tune himself up to a pitch where he hit the truth exactly. But at other times he was unable to resist the 'adjustment' of detail. He didn't lie in order to deceive, and not often to save his bacon. He lied to make things more like they ought to be: more amusing, sadder, more romantic, more strange, less humiliating. The lies could be as trivial as a description of a dinner's being delicious when in fact it was bad; it was their pointlessness, even more than the masterly naturalness with which he told them, which made them hard to spot, and in the end made me stop trying to spot them: that, and the knowledge that I was as likely to be doing him an injustice by suspecting a lie as I was to be fooled by believing one.

For one of them I am grateful. Didi was ten years younger than I am, but he passed himself off as eight years younger than that, and did so with great thoroughness, even to altering the date of his birth on his papers. 'Oh lord!' I said to him soon

33

after we met, 'eighteen years difference! I really *am* old enough to be your mother.' He answered impatiently: 'Don't be absurd, age means nothing. Don't you realize that you are far younger mentally and physically than most women in their early thirties?'

I am grateful that our relationship began with me being 'old enough to be his mother' because I fell in love with him the second time we met. A few days after my dinner party he took me out to show me the places which had become most precious to him during his student days, and sitting beside him in a small Hampstead pub I knew that I was in danger.

I was 'in danger' because I already had a lover of five years' standing who suited me perfectly and was more profoundly valuable to me than any other man could be. Not for a moment did I suppose that I would reach the point of wanting to break with Luke, but I might want to deceive him and that would be so unnatural between us that it would make me unhappy. It would be impossible for me to *love* little goat-face better than I loved Luke – but 'falling in love' has little to do with love, and I was startled to be reminded of how intoxicating it can be. The sensations involved are, after all, undeniably delicious: not least the sensation of danger, of being aware of risk and of a sudden release from one's inhibitions against embracing risk. 'Careful! This is likely to end in a painful mess ... But *so what if it does!*' It is exhilarating.

I was, however, 'old enough to be his mother', and in that knowledge lay sobriety. I find the spectacle of a woman throwing herself at a man who doesn't want her distressing and shaming. There is no good reason why I shouldn't find the sight of a man throwing himself at a woman who doesn't want him equally distressing, but I don't. Conditioning is irreversible. I can no longer remember exactly how I was conditioned, but conditioned I was: a woman should be the pursued, not the pursuer, her dignity depends on it. And how could a charming young man who could obviously take his pick of girls want a woman old enough to be his mother, who wasn't even beautiful? He couldn't, of course. Didi's true age would have been enough to chasten me, but it was the word 'mother' which made it conclusive.

From the start, therefore, I knew that any 'in love' sensations I experienced over Didi must be treated as a passing fever, and I meant 'treated' in the medical sense. They must be cured as soon as possible.

There are some advantages in growing older. I have learnt from experience, for example, that the mere recognition (if it is real) of hopelessness in being in love, and of the necessity of curing it, works as an important step towards recovery. In this case recognition would probably be all the treatment necessary. Provided I kept it in the front of my mind I could go on seeing Didi, and enjoying him, and although I must expect to suffer twinges for some time they would gradually fade away. The words I used to myself were: 'I shall be able to keep the pleasures of the friendship element, and make the rest change gear from the amorous to the maternal.' And that, exactly, is what happened.

Didi helped me by more than his deception over his age. He answered warmly to my friendship but he made it clear that he wanted nothing more. I am not the type of woman to whom he was attracted. The quality which always caught him was what he called 'elegance'. Surprisingly, considering how good he was at being elegant himself, the women in whom he saw it were sometimes quite inelegant in other people's eyes, but I learnt to recognize them. They had to give him the impression of being assured, cool, perhaps unattainable. Ideally they were dark and slim, deliberately 'feminine', and wore a lot of black. Their clothes were important. A 'little black suit', which in Western Europe deteriorated long ago to being the uniform of the tart on the one hand and the French governess on the other, and then all but disappeared, retained its status as a hallmark of elegance much longer on the shores of the Mediterranean – perhaps retains it still? A 'little black suit' on a dark slim woman was enough in itself to make Didi fall in love. I am not a 'little black suit' woman. I am fair, was already putting on weight by the time he met me, dress comfortably rather than smartly, and appear even more accessible than I am: few women have less 'mystery' than I have. Even if we had been the same age, Didi could not have fallen in love with me, and from the beginning he let me know him well enough to understand this.

A few weeks after we first met, on the last evening before he returned to Germany, we went out on a pub-crawl with friends of his and got drunk together. He was staying in my flat, after Dolly's return to Egypt. He had been hesitant about accepting my invitation, having sensed at once that I was attracted to him and fearing complications, but I had then introduced him to Luke and he had taken the introduction as I meant him to take it: I was safely back on the right side of the line and this was the signal for friendship. It may have been partly this which made him hold my hand on the way home that last evening – any withdrawal by a woman, even one he didn't want, was likely to make him advance – although by that time he had started to feel real affection for me, which was heightened by his misery at having to leave his beloved London next morning.

I had often noticed with rueful amusement his scrupulous avoidance of any physical touch, and I had drunk enough, and was enough moved by his unhappiness and the prospect of losing him to make much of this hand-holding. At that early stage the steadiness of my good sense depended almost entirely on its not being tested, and no more than this was needed to make it wobble. If he was prepared to hold my hand, perhaps ... I turned my palm to his and allowed all the sensuality I could muster to flow into the contact.

'Now then, sweetie,' said Didi, laughing. 'What would Luke think?'

'I don't care.' Just this once, I was thinking. It *can* only be this once, after all, he's going tomorrow, and I know I can get my balance back, so why shouldn't I have this one delicious collapse into abandonment?

He dropped my hand as soon as we were in the house and let me go up the stairs ahead of him, while he switched off the lights behind me. That told me nothing more would follow, but I was unwilling to accept it. As soon as we were in the flat he went to the kitchen to prepare our last 'midnight feast' – we had been forming a habit of late suppers of Egyptian food which he enjoyed cooking. We ate at a low table in front of the fire, sitting opposite each other, talking easily. I admonished myself to relax and not to mind that nothing more was going to happen, but I was still half hoping that the emotion of this fare-well occasion might end in love-making.

After the meal he cleared it away, came back to his chair and sat in silence for a few moments, leaning back, his eyes half shut, his expression deeply sad. Then he said suddenly: 'Oh god, Diana, I don't know that I can stand losing all this.'

I was up and across to him in one movement, without any thought, down on my knees beside him with my arms round him, kissing him. He didn't move, didn't even turn his eyes to look at me.

'Oh darling . . . ' I said, and kissed him again.

He still didn't move, only said gently: 'Sweetheart, you know I can't make love to you, you know it.'

And I knew it. I went on holding him for a moment or two, stroking the hair away from his forehead with one finger, then I said: 'Yes, I do know it. It's a pity, though.'

He gave a little laugh, and I stood up. I felt horribly dis-appointed but hardly at all rebuffed. Whether because of his gentleness or my own resilience, it didn't occur to me that his not wanting to go to bed with me when I wanted to go to bed with him would change our affection for each other.

'Oh well, love, I suppose it's time for bed,' I said. 'I shan't get up early tomorrow to say goodbye, it would be too sad.' Then I kissed him again and went to my room.

He thought that he had hurt me badly that night. 'How terr-ibly I must have hurt and humiliated her,' he wrote in his diary. 'How dreadful that night must have been for her.' Later there were to be times when I would have taken a sardonic pleasure in telling him that he was wrong, but now I am glad that he never knew that I went to sleep at once, as I normally do, and woke next morning feeling grateful to him because thanks to him the cure had just taken a big step forward and at this rate I would soon be over it. He needed, sometimes, to feel that he had hurt people. He didn't enjoy making people unhappy – he hated it – but at the same time the belief that against his will he had done so acted occasionally as a piece of string or a safety-pin in the groggy mechanism by which he hung on to his self-esteem.

I wasn't over it so very soon. For almost all the first year I knew him, the sight of one of Didi's letters on the doormat could make my heart jump in the way which only happens when one is in love, and certain things – the sound of a small Volkswagen's motor, and the taste of salad as Didi dressed it, for instance – continued to move me as though they were significant long after I'd become thankful that there was nothing for them to signify (I still sometimes pause to salute them even now). By the time of our meeting in Bruges I knew that I had been right, and that a maternal kind of concern was quite certainly taking over from amorousness, but even then the latter flickered up and coloured my response to him. That was, however, its last flicker. Simultaneously I moved a step nearer to understanding how seriously disturbed his whole personality was, and that was the true end of 'being in love'.

If my heart had never jumped at the sight of Didi's letters, if I had never wanted him physically, if I had never romanticized him, our relationship would not have endured. Sex and the maternal impulse are closely interwoven, particularly in childless women of middle age. However much I had liked a girl, and however great the girl's need, I would not have 'taken her on' as I was to take on Didi, nor would I have done it for a man to whom I had not, at first, been physically attracted.

The desire for children and sorrow at its frustration have never haunted me to the point of discomfort, but I am normal and healthy and I did at one time decide to have a child. Becoming pregnant early in my forties, I discovered that I wasn't – as I had thought at first – dismayed, but was jubilant. I would be able to support a child and I loved this one's father: I would let it be born. The months following this decision were the most intensely happy I have ever known, and when for no apparent reason I miscarried, it was only the seriousness of the miscarriage which prevented me from suffering badly. As it happened it almost killed me: a curious event to see as lucky, but the joy I experienced on coming round from an operation and discovering that I was still alive after bleeding almost to death was so overwhelming that it did much to counter-balance my grief at losing the child.

This attempt seemed to purge me of any wish to repeat it, but no doubt it defined the area of emptiness in the emotional life of any childless woman, and I have been more subject since then than I was before to the attraction of other people's need. To be able to feed, house and comfort someone: earlier I hadn't much impulse to do these things, but now I enjoy them. I like being turned to and relied on, I like being seen as indulgent, understanding and reassuring – a motherly figure. Whenever I was pregnant I was always sure that I was either preventing or – that one time – expecting the birth of a boy, and it is men, not women, whom I tend to mother. Having never had a son I cannot be sure to what extent sex would have coloured motherhood, but judging by the extent to which motherliness now colours sex in my relations with young men whom I find attractive, I suspect that it would have done so strongly – that I might have been quite a Jocasta, given the chance.

Elderly women in love with younger men are usually seen as pathetically greedy old cunts, avid only for love-making, desperately trying to nurse a fantasy of continuing youth and desirability in order to get it. Some of them may be like this, but some, I am sure, are in pursuit of a different kind of satisfaction. The silly old woman who gives her gigolo a gold cigarette case or jewelled cufflinks is possibly not only bribing him to continue fucking her but is also indulging her own pleasure in making him happy as she once made – or would have liked to make – a child happy by a present of a bicycle or roller-skates.

The give-away, surely, is that it is rare for an old woman to take on an impeccable young man. She couldn't do it, of course, since an impeccable young man would avoid being taken on, but she isn't often moved to do it. An impeccable young man finishes the jobs he undertakes, gets to appointments on time, doesn't buy silk shirts unless he can afford them, stays sober when he ought to, keeps himself clean. He is able to look after himself and creates no illusion that she is needed. The peccable young man, on the other hand, appears to create the state of affairs which exists between a mother and a child. She may at any moment have to rescue him because he has done something the equivalent of sticking his finger into a light socket, tearing his pants, skinning his knees, grabbing a toy which isn't his, being run over, getting lost. He goes straight to her need to be needed. And in addition, here is a child who is not a child, with whom it is at least *possible* to express the incestuous impulse which has to be repressed with a real child. If he should let her take his head in her hands, smell his hair, kiss away the hurt, he might well respond – as she mustn't let a child respond – by thrusting his way back towards her empty womb. That the situation is really far more complicated, and that she is the victim of illusion, makes it inevitable that if she becomes involved in such a relationship, much painful stumbling over knobbly truths will follow – but that, after all, is true of many forms of love.

Being less silly than some women, I was able to escape from falling too far into unseemly love with Didi, but it was a near thing, and that in spite of my being armed not only by his lie about his age and his sexual coolness towards me, but also – and far more strongly – by the existence of my real love for another man. It was impossible for me – and I always knew it – to go overboard for Didi in any fatal way; yet I found myself near enough to the edge to believe that I was given a glimpse of the nature of such affairs, and can now speak of them with some authority.

I know, therefore, that there was still a good deal of self-indulgence in my continuing affection for him after the last twinges of 'being in love' had died away. When I spent hours answering the desperate letters he wrote from Germany, counselling and consoling, encouraging and commiserating, I was certainly trying to help him but I was enjoying myself as I did so. I began to see how true this had been when answering his letters started to feel like a task. Counselling and consoling become fatiguing when you see that they aren't doing any good, and even when all I had actually seen of Didi was contained in two visits he had made to London of a few weeks each and our meeting in Bruges, the difficulty of helping a depressive was becoming evident. There is not much satisfaction in being kind and wise if it's all so much water off a duck's back.

When this thought began to sneak out from the back of my mind, I stopped to take a look at my own motives. It appeared that I had landed myself with more than I had bargained for, but I had to admit that *I* had landed *myself* with it. Didi, once he felt he could trust me, had grasped eagerly at what I was offering, but he hadn't forced it out of me, he had only accepted what I wanted to give.

That being so, I couldn't withdraw it. I had been enjoying myself in trying to make him less unhappy, and I had been enjoying myself in behaving as the sort of woman I would like to be: concerned, affectionate, kind and reliable, someone to whom a desperate man could safely hold. So if I wasn't going to puncture my own favoured image of myself, concerned, affectionate, kind and reliable I had damned well got to continue to be. It was an exhausting thought. I remember particularly being exhausted by it in my bath that Friday night when I admitted to myself that Didi was a 'nut': something which I kept out of the 'portrait' because that was supposed to be objective.

Didi's depressive crises had to relate to a woman. There had been Inge, there had been Ursula, and now there was Gudrun. She had been appearing as a minor character in his letters for some time. She was 'poor Gudrun' because she was in love with him: a sweet-natured girl who stayed behind after parties to help him wash up, inadequate in the role of *femme fatale*. It must have been the lack of anyone 'elegant' which made him use her.

Gudrun was happy when they became lovers. She had no wish to be 'complicated' or to torment him, so he had to do what he had done with Inge: force her to reject him so that he could long for her. He didn't do this consciously. Her compliance made her at first boring to him, then even sexually repulsive to a point where he found that she smelt disagreeable (he often found this about women: 'Like so many women I have known, she suddenly breaks out in a horrible smell – her mouth, her body, everything – at the moment of her climax'). He would be unable to disguise his revulsion; hurt and unhappy, she would withdraw; then the agonizing longing could begin. This time even Didi himself was unable to pretend that the girl had much to do with the tedious ritual. He was beginning to see that the girls never had much more connection with it than those feminine names given to hurricanes have with hurricanes: 'Inge', 'Ursula', 'Gudrun' – names for crises. So it didn't much matter that the present girl was particularly inappropriate – poor Gudrun! – for the role, and it certainly didn't prevent the crisis from being the worst yet.

Lying hour after hour, getting now and then, like a blow, a terrific crunch on my skull, a spasm of depression, of loneliness, of yearning, of absolute horror. I stand up, open the window, close it, walk up and down, close my eyes, open them, even feel nausea. As though caged, imprisoned in this infernal life. No one is to blame. This makes it even worse. A disease, an affliction ...

To go mad – as eventually I must as a natural antidote to this – to go mad slowly, alone, and aware of it must surely be a terrible torment. Sometimes I think of the Jews in concentration camps and compare my state to theirs – but suffering is all relative I suppose ...

I cannot *foresee* happiness any more. If this present depression is because of Gudrun, and if tomorrow Gudrun declared her love for me, that would still not make me happy ...

This time he went to a doctor ('He didn't laugh because I had warned him, but he smiled') who told him that his health insurance didn't cover psychiatric treatment, but who tried to help him with drugs. The pills worked for an hour or so at a time, but as soon as their effect wore off he was back in his pit, and he soon gave them up for the reason (an odd one in a man so given to addiction) that he feared becoming dependent on them. The doctor also encouraged him to probe his own condition, but this was no help.

Falling – falling – falling. Perhaps I have been unable to touch my diary lately, except in short fits, because at times I am repulsive to myself, I don't want to touch me, to interest myself in me. It is horrible to dislike your own self so much and there must be a vestige of genuine madness in all this (we have, alas, used the word 'mad' again). I look here, I look there for the cause of this misery, but I know what it is, it is 'love', this sickness. Anyone reading this diary will realize, as I do myself alas, the picture: a man in his thirties with the emotions of a schoolgirl. And very aware of it. But how to change? Is change possible now? Of course it isn't.

On Saturday stopped at midday for a drink at a pub, with a meal in view at home later, a fag and then sleep. Drug myself to sleep simply because I do not want to be awake. I was in that pub and I picked up a magazine. In it was a quiz, by -- I think – a psychologist, asking you questions which you answer and accord yourself points. The questions were about your ability to be in love – to love. So I answered the questions as truthfully as I could, added up my score and it came to 32. Then I turned to the summing up of your character according to your score. This is what it said: 'It is impossible, it is unbelievable – anyone scoring 34 points or less is still in his puberty as far as love is concerned.'

Yes. Yes ...

There is nothing I would welcome more than death at this moment, this very instant – here and now. How can I put it, and to whom? How can I express what I am going through to anyone but myself? Now I know I am diseased, that it is nobody's fault, that I have matured physically and also mentally except in one part of my brain coupled with a part of my feelings – particularly my emotions, which haven't matured at all. These two parts, a part of my brain and all my emotions, are in the same state they were in when I was seven or eight. If only they had shrivelled and died – but no, they remain young and fresh. Too too often I am at the mercy of their young power, their freshness which overpowers everything else in me, and I am left in this hopeless state of seeing myself, in my thirties, intelligent, terribly self-aware, overpowered by the feelings of a child. This exhausting fight, my mature reasoning self fighting desperately to get the upper hand, but succumbing despairingly in the unequal struggle – and I am left with what I am left with now: hopelessness, self-pity – an ugly and repulsive self-pity – and such despair, sadness, loneliness and finally utter darkness. Relief, o Lord, relief. There is nothing for me but to get drunk tonight . . .

I have no affection or respect for myself at all. I loathe and find intensely repulsive a man of my sort. I want to get out of my skin – it must be like a woman who has to put up with the embraces of a husband she loathes – that is how I feel about myself.

Day after day, week after week, month after month it continued. At times when he couldn't face the diary he wrote to me. He told me most of what he was going through, but because he was writing to be read by someone else he was able to introduce saving touches of irony, and what was reflected back to him from the letters was less frightening than what was reflected back from the diary, in the way that a mirror is less frightening to a sick woman – can even make her feel better – when she has been able to put on make-up. What we hung on to in our letters was that this was an illness, and that it would pass. If he could only endure, it would go away. When he was most ashamed of himself, and he was very ashamed ('My moaning, my endless whining') I told him, and meant it, that he was brave. And he *was* brave, ploughing his lonely way through this morass of despair and self-loathing, hanging grimly on to a purely formal, unfelt knowledge that the world, and himself, would look different if only he could survive.

That time, anyway, it was because I was there that he didn't kill himself. I was outside both the situation and the place where he was experiencing it, so I offered an alternative to death.

I am going to ask something which I know I shouldn't. Get me to London. It is unforgivable to ask it because as you know very well I shall not have a penny and it means you will be keeping me, but if I could be in London for three months or so I'm sure I could get round this work permit thing and find a job and then I'd be all right. This place is killing me. If I have to stay here I can't not kill myself.

I cabled 'Yes of course', and then thought: 'Oh my god!'

If Didi were to be given a visa for more than a holiday visit, he would need a work permit. To get a permit he would need an employer, and the employer would have to convince the Home Office that it was impossible to find a native qualified to do the job.

The law was clearly intended to protect the native's chances of employment against undercutting by foreigners ready to work for low wages, and to prevent foreigners from becoming a charge on the state. Since this was reasonable, it seemed likely that the Home Office would be reasonable towards someone who offered no threat. If a writer needed to be in England to finish a book, he would be doing no one out of anything; and if someone undertook financial responsibility for him he would cost the state nothing. So I applied for a permit for Didi, undertaking to ship him back to Germany if the authorities decided not to renew his visa. It was possible, after all, that once he came out of this crisis he *would* finish his second book in England. Given this start, Didi could then look for a job in which he could support himself and for which a permit could be granted, whereupon he could exchange the one I had procured for him for another more genuinely useful. Meanwhile he could no doubt find odd jobs – translating, baby-sitting, decorating? – for which he could be paid in cash without the Home Office's being any the wiser. It would be illegal for him to take such jobs, but I can't say that I felt any scruple at the idea of helping him to do so.

The permit was granted without trouble, but it took time simply because any dealings with the Civil Service take time. It was two months before I received the final confirmation, but they were encouraging enough from the start for me to tell Didi that the omens were hopeful, and I felt that having escape to

45

look forward to would do almost as much for him as coming to London at once would have done.

This was true. He was soon reporting that he had 'become a human being again', and gaiety and humour returned to his letters. He didn't, however, go back to his job, from which he had been absent on sick leave, and although he wrote about events again, not only about his mood, he gave no explanation of how he was living. He began to sound busy, but without describing any specific business, and I was puzzled over what he was up to. He was spending a lot of time in Düsseldorf, where he had made a new friend.

This friend, Peter, delighted him. For the first time in all his years in Germany he had met someone whom he could love rather than merely find agreeable. Peter was young, at odds with his family in some way, generous, intelligent, amusing, natural, 'un-German', and had a large library which contained all the books Didi loved best. They enjoyed the same reading, shared the same political convictions, laughed at the same jokes; and perhaps the best of all was that Didi was able to feel that he was contributing something good to Peter's life which had been lacking. He wrote a great deal about Peter, and a little about a kind and gentle girl to whom Peter had introduced him and with whom Didi was having an affair.

This picture emerged only gradually. Didi's ostensible reason for not coming to London as soon as the permit was granted was that he hoped to raise some money first by selling a television play on which he had been working, but I began to suspect, from a curious 'airiness' of tone which appeared in his letters, that this was not the whole truth. It looked as though, once the climax of his crisis was past with his desperate appeal to me and my response to it, he had started to enjoy himself enough to be reconciled with Germany – and to do this while being kept by Peter and the girl.

I found myself split-minded over this. I was relieved, but I was also cross. Commonsense told me to act on the relief – in other words, to leave well alone and make no attempt to remind him of my invitation – but inwardly I grumbled. It had not, after all, been a light decision to 'take him on', and I had been to some trouble to procure his permit; come to think of it, muttered the inward voice, it had been quite *generous* of me to do what I had done, and now the little wretch was preferring someone else's generosity. Of course one doesn't want *gratitude*, I told myself, but still ... but still ... And then the voice of commonsense: Oh come off it, thank your stars if he doesn't come after all, you know quite well what a problem he would be if he did. That was the first of many a long spell of inward muttering that I was to go through in the next three years.

Two or three months after the permit had been granted, by which time commonsense had won, Didi wrote to say that he would be with me in six weeks. In an 'Oh well!' mood, I bought a camp bed and a sleeping bag and emptied a drawer in the sitting-room bureau – my spare room, which I usually let, was occupied at the time, and Didi would have to camp – and this improved my temper. Preparing for a guest is pleasant in itself, and it reminded me how enjoyable Didi had been in that role before. I am out all day, and I knew from experience that he would be out most evenings, so his sleeping in the sitting-room would not be inconvenient, and since he was obviously well out of his crisis, his company when I had it would be gay.

A few days before he was to arrive, he sent the following letter:

Dearest sweetheart – Hm, hm, hm ... Hold your breath, sweetie ... because I find the whole thing terribly *funny*. Yesterday I was at the British consulate for my visa ... and I was *refused* – REFUSED – a visa!!!! My initial perplexity (and anger for ten minutes) gave way to a long laugh.

'But why?' I ask. – 'We must write to England first.' – 'I must know why.' – 'I am sorry' – the clerk is a nice man who stutters a bit and is very polite and is himself perplexed. 'It is the consul,' he says. – 'But I want to know WHY?' – 'Sorry.'

He went on to complain that he had got rid of his room and sold his car to a man who had insisted on making a profit when he let Didi have it back ('It is impossible to be *here* without a car'); this refusal of a visa had caused him so much inconvenience and expense, besides being cruel and unreasonable, that he was now in a fit of Anglophobia and quite *glad* not to be coming; and I wasn't to worry because although it would have killed him if it had happened while he was ill, now he had recovered he could stand it.

It was clear from the tone of the letter that the refusal was no disaster to Didi, but it puzzled and angered me because I had been told definitely that now he had a work permit he would get a visa without trouble. 'They' mustn't be allowed to get away with this, and I telephoned the man at the Home Office with whom I had been dealing. I was angry, he was puzzled and apologetic. He would call me back when he had looked into it. When he did so his voice was cold. There had evidently been some mistake, he said, because the visa had *not* been refused. The applicant had been told that it would be three or four days before he had it, which was customary, but that was all.

For a moment I thought that Didi had made the whole thing up, so that he could stay in Germany without hurting my feelings by admitting that he wanted to do so; then, reading his letter again, I suddenly saw what had happened as surely as if I had been in the consul's office at the time. He hadn't made it up – not consciously: he had simply *heard* the words spoken by the clerk as refusal. To get what he wanted he had not misrepresented, but had misinterpreted.

And this was, in fact, what he had done. Much later I was to read his diary account of the incident, and sure enough, he thought the visa had been refused and raved at the 'bloody limey authorities' who, he could see, had enjoyed refusing, and at the expense and inconvenience to which he had been put. The only part of his story to me which was a conscious lie was the tale of having sold his car and being forced to buy it back for more than he got for it. He hadn't sold it, although he had let his flat. In his diary he was on the very edge of seeing the trick he had played on himself – he admitted that he was pleased to stay in Germany and wrote 'no wonder!' on reporting that he'd had a tart letter from me – but he still contrived, by a hair's breadth, to believe himself a victim of a Kafkaesque bureaucracy.

My letter was tart because, having seen what he was up to, I wanted to end the situation. I told him that he had made a stupid mistake and that his visa was there for the taking, but that if he didn't want to take it there was no reason why he should. And as he clearly didn't, why not stop this play-acting and admit as much? It didn't matter to me whether he came to England or not, but uncertainty was inconvenient so if he had decided not to come would he please let me know.

I expected him to reply either by admitting that he was now happy in Germany, or with a flurry of hurt feelings and indignation, but his answer was perfunctory and airy: 'I think, sweetie, that you are being just a tiny little bit unfair ...' Perhaps the clerk in the consul's office had made a mistake, and of course he wanted to come – how could I suppose otherwise? – but just at the moment he did have rather a lot of things to settle.

My idea of a depressive was of someone who has spells of illness and who, between those spells, reverts to being 'normal'. It was to be some time before I would begin to understand how far out of kilter such a personality is all through, and that the crises of despair and self-disgust are only parts of a crippled whole. I suspected that Didi was living on his friends in Düsseldorf, but I didn't then know that he was also on a feverish gambling and drinking jag; and I had a good many other things to think about besides him. Retrospectively I can see the incident at the consulate, and the situation which led up to it, as a clear indication of his condition, but at the time it seemed no more than irritating and odd, and my reaction to feeling irritated and puzzled was to dismiss it as a waste of time. When, some two months later, in June 1966, Didi at last arrived in England, I had no trouble in forgetting how annoying he had been.

Didi made this easy. He had come, finally, because he had again been moved to come. The part of him which loved London and which trusted it as a place – the only place – in which he could feel at home and happy had surfaced again, and he made a festival of his arrival, radiating pleasure and affection. His power to project his moods was exceptional: all his friends recognized it. To decide that you would ignore what Didi was feeling was a waste of time, and when what he was feeling happened to be good, a perverse one because it meant rejecting genuine pleasures.

Didi had charm, and charm is not a trivial quality. It is a way of responding. People who have it make what they are regarding (and that includes you if they are regarding you) more vivid and enjoyable, funnier, more interesting, because that is how they find it. However mechanical charm becomes, and it does often become mechanical with exploitation, it is always to begin with a spontaneous quality. Didi's had not become mechanical. He often knew he was exercising it and sometimes deliberately exploited it, but even then it gave him so much pleasure that the freshness was preserved. He could cut it off, but when he did that he was depriving himself more than he was punishing others. There were to be angry times when I would say to myself 'He has nothing to recommend him but his charm: when he suppresses that there is nothing left.' I would be saying more than I knew. I would think that I meant only that his one virtue was a petty one, but in fact that virtue sprang from the centre of his being and was the thing about him which had enabled him to write with originality and truth. When it left him it was as though he went blind. On his arrival in London he was overflowing with it.

Having Didi in the house: footsteps running up the stairs, bringing a funny story. 'Listen, this is true, I swear it. I looked at her and I thought she may be mad but there's something serene about her – something sort of *holy*, and I whispered to L. all right, she's mad, but I believe because she'll be in the car, all the traffic lights are going to be green. And they *were* – every traffic light between London Airport and Kensington! So she said God always does such things for her and it was God who brought us together, so I must edit her book, I must. And L. said quickly "He's very busy with his own work, you know, it would be very expensive to get him to edit your book." And she said "Would a thousand pounds be enough?" I nearly fainted –

well, you can imagine! – and I said very nonchalantly with no breath in my voice, oh well, I supposed ... And she had this sort of shopping bag on her knee, and she pushed her hands into it and took out *a thousand pounds in dollars*.'

'Didiiii! Show me – show me at once!'

'Are you mad? How could I take them, how could I do such a thing? No, we were scared, L. and I, it was too mad, all those traffic lights and everything. We said we must make a proper contract, and I must do a sample bit before she decides – we became very sober and virtuous, it was terrible.' (Part of me knew, of course, that the holy lady would never be mad *enough*, but Didi could always make things seem possible.)

Or I would come home and find a tray in the sitting-room with 'a little aperitif' all ready: cubes of cheese, radishes cut into roses, celery feathery in a glass and salted almonds roasting in the oven. 'Do you want help in the kitchen, Didi?' – 'No, what are you thinking of! You know me.' Exchange of news through the door open between sitting-room and kitchen while he, with a flowered apron of mine round his middle, performs alchemy with three courgettes, a pound of mince and a bechamel sauce. 'Is Didi in a cooking mood? Is he making one of his delicious creamy things?' says Luke when he arrives, and Didi calls 'Don't tell him, it's to be a surprise' – then darts in with a lettuce: 'Look, what beautiful salad I found in the market – *look* at it.' He never mixes a dressing in advance. When the salad is in the bowl he grinds the pepper over it, scatters salt, sprinkles oil and lemon juice, pausing every now and then to bend over it and inhale its smell to see how near perfection he has come – no, a few more grinds of pepper, another drop or two of lemon. Luke has gone into the kitchen and started to pick and nibble. Didi drives him out, crying 'Stop him! He's ruining his appetite – ' then sees that I am smoking and exclaims in despair 'You're both hopeless.' A little later he comes through the door without the apron, an almost tranced expression on his face. '*Now*,' he says, '*now* we can start opening our appetites,' and he pours himself a drink with ritual gravity and walks about the room as he takes the first sips, his eyes half closed to concentrate his senses. Didi's appetite can be opened by things which would close most people's for the night such as the best part of a bottle of whisky or several pints of beer (he has probably had the beer already before coming home to cook), but to see him now you would think him a gourmet of impeccable chastity, savouring one glass of dry sherry for the meal's sake; and however unorthodox his methods, his appetite *is* opened. He eats as though he were reading a poem.

Then there is the pleasure of sitting on the floor by Luke's chair, relaxed against his knee, while Didi, who is making us laugh, looks at us with tenderness. He is loving us, romanticizing and simplifying us as he does so delightfully to those he loves with affection, and so disastrously to those he loves with passion. In his eyes we are being lovable Luke and sweetheart Diana: dear, gentle, funny, trusting people (slightly childish in our trustingness – he has to look after us), with a touching relationship. He enjoys sharing jokes and ideas with us, and he admires Luke's writing, but he loves us as 'characters' more than he likes us as companions; and we, sitting opposite him, accept our roles smugly, if slightly sheepishly. It makes us feel very *nice*. And we are relaxed because we know that at just the right moment Didi will get up and leave, saying that he has arranged to meet so-and-so, he is late already.

Perhaps afterwards, when we are in bed, he will make us laugh again, although this time it will be at him, not with him: we know that although he loves us he also considers us in some ways barbaric. He leaves his diaries in a pile on the table he has to share with me, shows us parts of them and knows that from time to time we leaf through other parts. We know that he has written of us: 'It's rather strange. They jump (I think) into bed at once, make love, or rather just fuck, and an hour later they are in the sitting-room again. I don't know which is better – this hello, fuck, cheers, or my terribly elaborate way, drinking and smoking and eating and leading up to it and music and lights etc. I prefer mine, of course – but then they don't have time, poor dears.'

'So that's what we do, love – "or rather, just fuck",' I say to

Luke. 'He's got a nerve!', and we hug each other and I feel sorrier for Didi than he feels for us.

Or there are Saturday mornings, my shopping mornings. Didi cooks only erratically, when he wants to express affection or to make an occasion seem important, but he drives me to the shops on Saturdays without fail, seeing it as a return for hospitality. We go to the market in Camden Town and to a Greek grocer in the market. We always mean to go early but rarely get there before midday, and soon we have a ritual, starting at the end of the street with a Guinness or two in the pub which smells of Lysol and is full of old Irishmen, then working our way down from stall to stall. We always pause to examine the junk stall and sometimes find a treasure – a pudding-basin for sixpence, and once, for half a crown, a beautiful photograph in faded sepia, heavily framed, of a dragoman showing the sphinx to Edwardian tourists, which Didi says might have come straight out of a railway station waiting-room in Egypt. We call at the toyshop, too, because Didi says that the man who runs it is a socialist: once, when we exclaimed at the cheapness of the toys, the man said 'Poor children need toys too, you know,' and we have liked it ever since and get all our presents for children there, and horrible bath-cubes because Didi insists that they are a bargain, and toothbrushes which cost sixpence and last about a fortnight. If we are in a hurry we split up and take the stalls separately, Didi getting the vegetables while I get the fruit and eggs, meeting again in the grocer's for the Greek bread, the olive oil, the tahina, the spices, all the things which need consultation. And finally we go to the butcher we like best because he has chalked on his window-glass 'MEAT BOUTIQUE AND RUMP STEAK EMPORIUM' and his fascia carries the mysterious words ' 'Tis not immortal to command success, but we do more deserve it.'

Didi greatly enjoyed picking up the threads of old friendships dating back to his student years in London, and making new friends, but he surprised me by being at first only intermittently happy, then not happy at all, to see again those of his relations who turned up in London from time to time. The loving mood of his visit to Dolly and Mémé seemed to have evaporated, and now the members of the family often found each other 'impossible'. Their image of the devotion which they felt for each other – and of what the other ought to feel for them – was extremely demanding: mothers ready to nourish children with the flesh of their hearts, children ready to sacrifice anything rather than bring a tear to a mother's eye. While they were cushioned by money and status in the society which produced them, it was perhaps easy to enjoy the luxury of believing in this image; but those of them who had been reduced, either by choice or by necessity, to the precarious condition of exile, seemed to me to come up pretty smartly against reality. Love flowed as freely as ever when it was no trouble, but could curdle into complaint and resentment overnight if it had to face claims.

I heard much from Didi on these curdlings in others towards himself, but I couldn't help noticing a similar process at work in him towards others. Only for one cousin, a girl much younger than himself who was having a hard time, did he continue to feel sympathy and love. There was little to choose between him and the rest of them when it came to disgust at another person's selfishness when something was being demanded of oneself. The only moral advantage he had over the rest of the family was that materially he had absolutely nothing over which to crouch jealously, while they had at least a little.

As I came to know more about people like those among whom Didi had been brought up, I realized that they – and particularly the women – are strange mixtures. Perfectly at home among the elegant and cosmopolitan in any part of the world, on the surface they belong less to a country than to an income-group: the rich. They do have a country, however, and it is one in which the women have only recently begun to be educated and become free to move out of the home. Their grandmothers certainly, and often their mothers, lived in a different age and by a different set of moral values. A part of Didi's family, anyway, was undergoing a double exile even before physically leaving Egypt: a voluntary exile from a way of life, and an involuntary exile from the world of the rich. It was not surprising that they felt that they had their work cut out to keep afloat themselves, and could spare little thought for anyone else. It had to be everyone for himself or herself.

What made the situation hard to understand at first was that they still spoke, and no doubt often felt, as though this were not so. They had always been addicted to generous emotions, so they went on expressing them. This was hard on Didi, who shared the addiction with the best of them and could never resist the luxury of believing loving words and gestures coming from the people from whom he most needed them – believing them, and sometimes inventing them, and then, when the truth emerged, becoming vicious in his pain and anger. I soon concluded that the idyllic elements in his childhood which he liked so much to describe were wished-for more often than they were remembered. This was not a family in which an odd-child-out with a difficult nature, and who was likely to be a financial liability, could be considered anything but 'impossible', and the rejection must have been even more thorough than I had thought. Dolly had done her best – of that I was sure, and Didi always insisted on it even when he was angriest with her; but even with Dolly love, when it came to the pinch, was by now more a matter of faith than of acts.

After a month had gone by Didi and I began to say to each other 'We really must start thinking about this job problem'; but we usually said it late in the evening when 'tomorrow' seemed the appropriate time for decisions. I felt that Didi deserved a holiday, and I had little idea what we were going to do. Presumably Didi would start scanning advertisements in the *New Statesman* and so on, and we would both ask around among friends, and if anything likely turned up I would produce a reference. I had thought of employing him in my office, but had rejected the idea as bound to lead to trouble. As a publisher's reader he would be good at detecting good writing, but he had no commercial sense; he would be looking for Chekhovs all the time, and would be unable to judge whether something he despised might be useful on our list. As an editor he was disqualified because he was slapdash about detail and although he could use English vividly and honestly, he was unable to spell it and was uncertain about its grammar. I could foresee the effect of this practical inefficiency combined with his arrogance about his opinions and his large areas of ignorance on my colleagues – and on myself – and although I knew that he was disappointed at my not offering him work (I explained to him why I couldn't), I was not going to risk it.

Then our neighbour downstairs, my cousin who owns the house, came to the rescue. Didi had declared himself ready to do anything, so diffidently she suggested that he might paint the hall and stairs. She found out what a professional decorator would charge, and offered to pay him this sum.

Didi responded as though painting the stair-well of a tall house would be a lark. This stair-well, he said, would be the most elegant in London, the walls white, the paintwork picked out in black – perhaps alternate black and white rails on the banisters? Neither my cousin nor I like paintwork picked out, but his delight in the idea made us feel that it would be unkind to resist it and we let him have his way. When asked whether he would prefer my cousin to buy the materials and to pay him simply for his work, or to give him the whole sum so that he could do the shopping for the job himself, he chose the latter. Let her give him £10 or £15 at a time, he said, and he would spend what seemed to be the right proportion of it on equipment and paint and keep the rest for wages, and see how far it took him. It might turn out that the materials cost less than we expected and then my cousin wouldn't have to fork out the full £80 that the decorators had said the job was worth.

He decided that first he must strip the walls – he couldn't make a good job of it unless he did. We told him that stripping would probably be harder work than he thought, and that it wasn't necessary, but he refused to listen. Energetically and cheerfully he began to strip the hall.

He managed that, and a few feet round the turn on to the stairs, before reality caught up with him and cheerfulness dwindled. It was an appalling job, particularly as he was saving money by not hiring proper ladders and planks, and on the third day he announced slightly accusingly and as though he were the first to discover it that to strip such an area of wall was a job for a professional and that it wasn't necessary anyway, so from now on he would just paint.

He began by using emulsion, but soon changed to whitewash because it was cheaper. He also began carefully, but then decided that if he applied the whitewash very thickly, with rough strokes, it would give the walls an interesting texture. He almost threw the stuff on to the wall, so that besides swirls and lumps there were long trails of dribble. ('Someone must have done this job with his feet,' said a house-painter the other day, but the effect is not disagreeable.) He also spread whitewash and black paint everywhere, so that I couldn't pick up a tea-spoon without getting paint on my fingers, and my carpets were tracked with painty footprints. 'It will come off,' he said impatiently, 'I'll do it when I've finished,' but he never did.

Soon he was talking about 'those bloody stairs' instead of about 'my stairs', and the only way he could face them was by doing very little at a time and often taking days off. It took him two months to finish, and cost my cousin considerably more than £80, although Didi came to feel that he had been paid too little because the longer he spun the job out, the further and thinner the money had to stretch.

Not that he attempted to stretch it. We soon realized that he always bought less paint at a time than he said he bought, and that he drank and gambled the money left over on the day he got it. 'She has no idea how much paint is needed,' he would then say to me in a worried voice. 'I don't know what to do. It's going to cost her much more than she thought, and she can't afford it, poor girl. I don't know how to tell her I need more paint already, it's horribly embarrassing.' But at the same time, because the money he made stayed in his pocket for such a short time, he felt that he had made none. The lark of painting the stairs had become a boring, fatiguing, unprofitable chore – and I began to question the picture of patient industry in humble tasks during his years in Germany which had moved me so much when I first met him.

Both my cousin and I knew that he was doing the job sloppily, that he was taking an absurd amount of time over it, and that he was cheating over his expenses; so why did we tolerate it?

It was partly because of an attitude we share about possessions: we are not house- or possession-proud women, we spend as little time and energy on housekeeping as we can, and neither of us has ever felt more than passing regret over objects lost or broken. If the stairs had been well done it would have pleased us; if they were done sloppily, too bad, but we would soon stop noticing it. And neither of us much minds being cheated, although naturally we would prefer not to be. It always seems to me, and I think to my cousin too, an embarrassing experience rather than a distressing one, and on the whole it's easier, as well as kinder, not to notice. We were brought up in families which maintained the strictest standards of honesty in all outward matters, and where no strain was put on those standards; and whereas we have both reacted against much that we were taught in our youth, this we seem to have absorbed to a point where we see anyone dishonest as deformed rather than sinful. This 'pretending not to notice' is foolish. It means that you lay yourself open to being cheated – invite it, almost – so if it happens, what right have you to complain? Both on the irrational level and the rational, therefore, it is something on which I cannot feel seriously indignant.

In addition to this, Didi was in a miserable position in having to depend on our charity. He knew that my cousin would not have had the stairs painted if she hadn't wanted to help him – he guessed it at once, and evidently disbelieved me when I denied it. It was possible for him, without too much loss of dignity, occasionally to 'borrow' money for petrol (he often used his car to help us) or for food, but he couldn't comfortably say 'Lend me £5, I want to get drunk tonight' or 'I've got the gambling urge.' Didi *had* to drink and gamble – that was how he felt about it, and that, I realized much later, was the literal truth. At the time I had not yet understood to what extent a neurotic person's 'symptoms' are his props, his techniques for endurance, pathetic ones certainly, but the only ones he can command; but I did already sense, and so did my cousin, that we must not expect Didi to be rational about drinking and gambling, and that it wasn't surprising if he tried to wangle a taste of them when given the chance.

Another element in our lack of indignation was the value which Didi soon developed as an object for observation and discussion: 'Guess what he's done now!' If he said he was going out for a quiet evening with friends, adding 'And it will *have* to be quiet, I've only got 3s 6d left', and I learnt later that he had instead gone to a gambling club and lost the best part of the £10 he'd just been given for paint, he was in a way offering us entertainment: indeed, the worse he behaved (within his really very modest range) the more interested and amused we would be. An appetite for gossip can stomach a good deal of inconvenience.

But our acceptance of his behaviour was not due only to our own natures. The power of Didi's personality contributed much to it. If he had come to feel that he was demonstrating virtue and strength of will in finishing a boring job, and was doing it only out of generosity to us, then he could make us feel it too. The power of the auto-suggestive process by which he generated his moods and interpretations of events was such that it spilt over on to other people – men as well as women, though women were more subject to it – who often found themselves astonished at the discrepancy between how they saw something when they were in his company and how they saw it when they thought about it later. It was to Didi's credit that he was not a serious con-man. He had the equipment for it, but he did no more than obtain a roof over his head, one meal a day, a little petrol for his car, his drink and (only in fits and starts) his gambling – the bare necessities of life, from his point of view – which showed restraint and goodwill towards his friends. He never had any truck with people whom he couldn't accept as friends (although, as I was to learn, he could have spells of finding his friends antipathetic); it would never have occurred to him to pretend friendship only for what he could get out of someone.

The rapid collapse of his good intentions over the stairs combined disturbingly with my random readings of his diary. It surprised me that he allowed these readings, because although they told me almost nothing I didn't already know in outline, they filled in the picture in a way painfully unflattering to him. I learnt, for instance, that what I had suspected about the period immediately before he came to London was true, and that he had been kept during that time by his friend Peter and the girl he was having an affair with – because, as he put it, 'it seems pointless and stupid to go and work for 2.50 DM an hour and then go and gamble, so I'm not working any more': reasoning all the more disconcerting because he was evidently unaware of its oddness. And I learnt with dismay how disabled he was in love.

'His capacity to love is deep and candid' I said of him in my portrait. His *longing* to love was deep and candid, and it is unlikely that such a longing, such a sense of the pre-eminent value of love, could exist in someone who wasn't born with a strong potential for loving. But where now was the capacity? I had thought that he destroyed trivial loves because he despised their triviality, and that his thirst for a great and true one was something which with luck he might assuage. But the more I read of his private accounts of his relations with women, the more doubtful I became. None of his affairs, apart from a small category of random fuckings when exceptionally drunk (which he loathed) were trivial. All of them were wild bids for something beyond him, and were doomed.

He never 'saw' the women he pursued; and when, after he had caught them, he had to recognize their individuality, he resented it. The magical creature would become 'a bore' – 'stupid' – 'mediocre' – 'neurotic'. Although he believed himself to be haunted and driven by sex ('I am unable to imagine love without sex' – 'It is always all sex with me, if I love her I want to fall on her every minute'), his own accounts made it clear that physical delight in itself meant almost nothing to him, perhaps even disgusted him. The passion which overtook him boiled in his head, and his head alone, in response not to an actual body but to a dream image which some single feature or some article of clothing had conjured up in him. As soon as a woman had been in his bed once or twice and he had been forced to apprehend the reality of her body, its shape and texture and smells, it would become repulsive to him, just as her personality became tedious to him once he had perceived it. Very quickly he would become unable to make love to her unless he was at least a little drunk, and the more often he had to do it, the drunker he had to be. The truth, I began to suspect, was that he could *never* make love sober: if he were not intoxicated by the quick flash of the romantic dream in his imagination, he had to be intoxicated by alcohol.

He knew this about himself, was always ashamed of it, and during his depressive crises was appalled by it, but he couldn't change it and at bottom he didn't want to change it. No other experience was so ravishing to his whole being as that quick flash of illusion, that momentary dazzle of being intensely alive, and it seemed to him that if he loved in any other way he would forfeit the very essence of joy.

Those early readings of passages here and there in his diaries were chilling. It was impossible not to see that my first idea of his illness had been inaccurate, and that he was to a large extent crippled even when he was 'well'. The question 'What will become of him?' now concerned me more closely than it had done before: he was in my house and on my hands — for how long? I could envisage no acceptable answer to it when I looked at the diary, so I preferred to look at Didi in the flesh: tiresome at times, of course, but healthy and gay, amusing and amused, a pleasure to have about and perhaps on the way to a real recovery. This was, after all, the first time for many years that he had lived in a place which could become his home, with people whose affection he might learn to trust. If he found a job in which he could use his languages and his intelligence, all might be well.

I began, therefore, to shy away from the diaries, although my shameless inquisitiveness would draw me back to them from time to time for a quick peep. It was a relief when one day Didi said that he'd started to feel uncomfortable at the thought of me and Luke reading them, and that he would rather we didn't any more.

I said all right, but we'd have to make a rule. Anything left lying about I was likely to look at – I might try not to, but I knew the strength of my impulse to pry and I couldn't count on controlling it. He knew that very well because he was the same, admit it now! He admitted it – we were both laughing – and we agreed that from then on we must both put away anything we wished to keep private. I could trust myself not to open a drawer or dig about in a suitcase. Whether I could trust Didi on that I was not so sure, but as I was unlikely to have any vital secrets I didn't mind.

From that day he kept his diaries hidden and I didn't read them again. Sometimes, when I suspected him of making a more than usually strange or comic 'adjustment' in his account of events, there would be a twinge of temptation to see how it compared with his private record, but I was able to withstand it. I was so familiar by then with his patterns of behaviour that they had lost their savour, so my restraint was not particularly honourable.

4 A Holiday Companion

That September, when Didi had been with me three months, we went to Yugoslavia. It was a holiday conceived in a moment of gaiety when we were having a drink with my cousin. Neither she nor I had yet decided where to go, and a Yugoslav friend of ours suddenly said: 'Why don't you all come to my place? There's plenty of room and I know my parents would like it very much.'

'Wonderful idea!' said Didi. 'I'll drive you all there in my little car.'

My cousin's husband couldn't get away, so the party was my cousin and her two-year-old son, our friend Ana, Didi and myself. In the end only Ana, Didi and I went by car, and the other two flew out to join us. Our plans were made in an effervescent mood, Didi cheerful and bustling as he had been at the prospect of painting the stairs.

This holiday suited me well, because I was in for a long cold winter. Luke had taken a job which would keep him abroad for eight months from the middle of September, and I was going to miss him badly: we had been lovers for seven years by then, seeing each other at least once a week and sometimes more, and in the peculiarly unromantic way we share, we had come to love each other more and more solidly. I would miss him badly, and I was thankful that we could leave for Yugoslavia the day after he went away, so that my mind would be taken off my loneliness. 'I'm glad', he said, at our goodbye meeting, 'that you're off on this gay holiday tomorrow and that you'll go on having Didi here to keep you cheerful.'

I had misgivings about Didi's pleasure in the holiday once we got there. The picture in his mind of the Mediterranean (as he insisted on calling the Adriatic) was coloured by memories of Cannes and Alexandria, and I remembered that in Belgium the places he had responded to most enthusiastically had been Ostende and Zeebrugge (nightmare places to me, but to him temptingly packed with bars and restaurants). Suspecting that his idea of what a small coastal town in Yugoslavia would be like was hazy, I thought I had better warn him that the only really good food we were likely to eat would be fish, which he happened to detest, and that the place would be stronger on nature than it would be on elegance.

He looked dismayed for a moment about the fish, but quickly pooh-poohed me. He was expert, he said, at finding delicious little restaurants, and there would always be the drink.

'But I thought you said slivovitz was the one drink you couldn't take?'

'It is, but what about the wine?'

'It will be all right, but not special.'

'Oh well, I can always be happy so long as there's draught beer.'

'I don't think . . . ' I began, but he interrupted me. 'Nonsense, of course there'll be draught beer . . . Ana, what's the beer like in your town? Is there a good draught beer?'

'I'm not sure,' said Ana, who didn't know what draught beer was. 'I didn't drink beer much at home, but I expect there is.'

'There you are!' said Didi.

Weakly, I dropped the subject of beer, but I went on to warn him that he might find the holiday dull in other ways: 'A holiday with two middle-aged women and a very small child – we'll have to gear our activities to the child, do you realize that?' Sweetly he answered that he could imagine no holiday more delightful than a restful one with my cousin and me and the child; and since he did, after all, know us and our ways very well, I could only assume that he knew what he was saying.

Didi had often driven from London to Dover, so we left our

starting plans to him. We must be ready to start at three o'clock in the morning, he said, so as to catch the early car ferry. With a considerable effort of will – I am very bad at early starts – I was up and ready in time, hoping that the others felt as little like talking as I did, and off we went.

Didi had surprised me by becoming fussed and old-maidish over packing and loading the car – I had expected him, after his nomad life, to be casual about such things – and he surprised me again as soon as we had started by asking how we got out of London on to the Dover Road.

'Surely you know? You've done it lots of times, and you know how hopeless I am about roads. Look at the map.'

He refused to look at the map, and took us out over the wrong Thames bridge. We saw from the signposts what had happened and I suggested the map again, realizing from the reluctance with which Didi gave way that he was going to be one of those tiresome drivers who see it as humiliating to admit ignorance of the route. We were becoming a touch irritable, but I put it down to the ungodly hour, and was glad to notice that we hadn't lost enough time to matter, and could be back over the river and on to the correct route within ten minutes. It was astonishing, therefore, when as we approached Westminster Bridge Didi jammed on the brakes and said 'Oh my god, look at that!'

'That' was the signpost on the bridge saying 'DOVER 78m.' 'Seventy-eight miles!' said Didi indignantly, as though this had been sprung on him as a malicious trick. 'We can't possibly do it in the time. We'll have to go back home and take the next ferry.'

I remember thinking of a row of asterisks and exclamation marks such as were used in old copies of *Punch* to indicate bad language. I couldn't explode – it would be too ill-tempered, too stupid to explode, what did it matter really, make yourself see it as funny for god's sake, and anyway *keep silent*. But the silence was crackling with ****!!! ****** ****!! ***** ******* *********!!!!!

Didi offered no apology. 'Oh well,' he said, 'it will be nice to get a bit more sleep,' and he seemed to emerge from his state of fluster into one of calm superiority to my silent rage.

We caught the next ferry and decided to make the first drive a short one and stay the night in Bruges. On the surface the day went by cheerfully, but I had started on a spell of inward muttering that morning, and I couldn't stop it. I was tired after a long year's work and had the depression following Luke's departure to contend with, so it was not surprising that my temper wasn't at its best, but still I felt ashamed of myself and that made it worse.

I already knew that the authoritative way in which Didi gave opinions or told facts didn't always mean that his opinions were sound or the facts true, and I was usually amused when I caught myself automatically believing him in spite of this, paying tribute to his masterly way of 'knowing best'. Now the kind of unreliability peculiar to him was becoming more evident with every minute, and it was mortifying to find myself suddenly unable to be amused.

To Didi in certain moods the trimmings of life were of serious importance: the quality of a restaurant, the way a meal was served. He could live happily on bread and cheese for weeks, and reacted with quick distaste to snobbery or vulgarity, but some aspects of good living held a special place in a corner of his imagination and he believed himself – declared himself – to have a special sensitivity to such things. He thought he could recognize at a glance the authentically good restaurant and the bar with genuine character, and it mattered to him that this was so. Shadows of his rich and cosmopolitan uncles stood behind him in these moods; he was proving himself as 'elegant' and 'worldly' as they were – or more so, because they had worked from experience while he was inspired only by the fineness of his 'aristocratic' instinct.

Now he was 'on the Continent' with two ignorant women. He had spent a good deal of time in Paris and had travelled widely, apart from living for ten years in Germany, while Ana had never left Croatia till she came to London, and I (I noticed with distinctly sour amusement) was automatically disqualified from being 'sophisticated' by being English. He felt that he could show us the places we were passing through, open our eyes to their true character – and he was almost always (oh my poor Didi!) wrong.

Neither Ana nor I was allowed much say in choosing the places where we would eat or sleep, and the restaurant in which we ended in Bruges was a good example of what we got. 'Now!' Didi had said, 'we are going to trust my instinct,' and he led us into the most obvious tourist trap in the town, its walls invisible behind reproduction copper warming-pans, blue and white china windmills and folksy sayings in poker-work, and the waiters peevish and overworked. When I ordered steak and chips I was thinking, the Belgians live on chips, so they can't go far wrong on those, but the chips were soggy and the steak had that repulsive cottony texture which betrays that its toughness has been beaten out of it with a heavy spiked instrument. It was impossible for Didi not to have recognized this – he had demonstrated his true feeling for food over and over again – but tonight he was knowing best and his 'instinct' had led us to this place, so the food had to be first-rate. He had the prudence to leave me out of it, but he turned to Ana: 'Just taste this, Ana! You see – now we are in a place where they really *know* food!'

Later that evening my bad temper surfaced and I couldn't resist saying to Ana 'That restaurant!'

'Let him enjoy himself,' said that kind, wise girl; and I agreed, feeling even more ashamed of myself. How could Didi be expected to know about such things? He had lived in Europe only as an impoverished student and a penniless exile, so he can hardly ever have eaten in a good restaurant – and what a pathetic and harmless little dream he was trying to bring to life. I resolved to 'let him enjoy himself' by keeping my mouth shut.

In the four days of the journey this resolution was put severely to the test. Not only was Didi naive about quality in restaurants and inns, but he was also (again not surprisingly) ignorant about European history and blind to European art forms and architecture. The authority with which he pronounced on whatever we saw remained unshaken on the surface, but he must have been uneasy underneath because he was prickly whenever I betrayed that I knew anything. This didn't happen often, because many things I didn't know, and a number of the things I did know I kept to myself once I had seen how he reacted; but whenever I was able to answer a question of Ana's, or said 'Oh look, there's such-and-such', I could feel him bristling. I was soon looking forward eagerly to the relaxation which would follow when at last we were released from the car, and our intimacy would be diluted by the presence of my cousin and her son.

I failed to realize at once that if I was becoming edgy it was nothing to what Didi was becoming, but I did see that the place disappointed him as much as I had feared it would. An austere and rocky landscape had no charms for him. Like most people raised in a country where nature is hostile, he disliked the wild and the barren and saw the typically English romantic response to it as a tiresome affectation. To my cousin and me, discovering 'a lovely beach' meant discovering a place where land went into sea with a special grandeur, and where there was *nobody else*; to Didi it meant discovering one where the amenities were conveniently and prettily arranged and where *the other people* looked attractive. There were plenty of our 'lovely beaches' in the neighbourhood, and none of his except for the pine-shaded town beach with its gay kiosks and umbrellas – and that was populated almost entirely by fleshy, middle-aged Germans and their children. Away from the beaches the country was poor, the villages shabby, the people – naturally enough! – peasants. Didi felt ashamed of himself for seeing only the drabness – he wanted to be excited by Yugoslavia because it was a Communist country – but drabness was what he saw; and he had so little sense of history, topography or the realities of politics that he could extract no interest from it. He was 'very disappointed' by Yugoslavia.

He found the women ugly, too. We were not in a part of the country where they are famed for their beauty, as they are in the region of Dubrovnik, and in Montenegro. Here they tended to be swarthy and stocky, and most of them were dressed in the dark and shapeless clothes of peasant women anywhere. There were some fine faces, but there was no 'elegance'. After one stroll round the town it was apparent that Didi had written the place off as far as women went.

Three weeks without romance and sex in a place where the sun was hot and the sea was blue would be sad for him, I could see; but I hoped he might not be too upset by it because until just before we had left London he had been having a high old time, and had seemed to be proving himself in a period of stability by taking it lightly. He had been running two simultaneous affairs with women who knew each other, one of which involved much daring husband-dodging – had, in fact, been behaving outrageously for the sheer sport of it, doing no harm to anyone more by luck than by judgment – and I had felt pleased about it. Because I myself, at times, had enjoyed just such light-hearted 'naughtiness' I saw it as sane compared to Didi's usual catastrophic romanticism, and congratulated myself that bringing him to London had already done him good. He ought to be able to survive for three weeks on the fat of these entertaining affairs.

But something had happened. It had happened very suddenly, showing itself first in his fluster at the start of our journey. I had been too full of my own irritation and my attempts to control it to notice it on the journey, and for the first two days after we arrived it was concealed by his reactions to the place. It was not until some time during the third day that I realized Didi had become abruptly unable to live on the fat of anything, and that he had also started to find me unendurable. I had, almost overnight, become so maddening to him that he could hardly bring himself to speak to me. If I asked a question he would answer it to my cousin or to Ana, and if he was unable to avoid addressing me he would do so briefly and often rudely, with averted eyes.

It was disconcerting, even shocking. Until only a few days before we had been on terms so easy and affectionate that they could not possibly have been based on anything but a genuine affinity, and I had been counting on him to understand my loneliness at Luke's departure and to cheer me up with his particular kind of loving gaiety. And now this!

I decided that my irritability on the journey must have penetrated my efforts to conceal it, and abraded his nerves. The best thing to do was for us to keep apart as much as possible for some days, and no doubt the mood would pass.

It was easy to go our separate ways. Each morning my cousin and I would decide which beach we wanted to go to. If it was one of the more distant ones we would ask Didi to drive us there and to fetch us later if he didn't want to stay, and we would spend the day swimming and sunning and playing with the child: not an exciting holiday, but a restful and pleasant one. In the evenings we would stroll into the town for a drink, asking Didi if he would like to come too because we were trying to overcome his mood by pretending not to notice it, and (since it showed no signs of lifting) feeling relieved when he said no. He spent much time in his room – 'I have some writing to do' – and went for lonely drives. On the few occasions when he came to the beach with us he would talk a little with my cousin and play with the child – he was consistently charming to the child, even on his worst days – but more often he would wander off and sit by himself, an aloof little figure with an expression of haughty melancholy on his face. 'Oh dear, what a bore he is,' said my cousin. 'It's like carrying round a little portable thunder cloud,' and it was. Didi's power of mood-projection was at its strongest. Even when he was shut in his room we could feel him there – and hear him, because he developed a raucous and tortured cough (he always did this when he was disturbed) with which to signal his gloom.

'What are we to *do* with him?' we asked each other. We tried to find an 'elegant' girl for him on the town beach, but without success; we tried sending him off to a casino in a nearby town, but that was a failure because the casino only accepted foreign currency and our money was in dinars.

The only occasions which he managed to enjoy were the evenings when we played darts with Ana and her family. He had taught Ana the game in London and they had decided to introduce it to Yugoslavia and had brought a board and two sets of darts with them. Ana's family took to it with enthusiasm and skill, and we played with the board fixed to a palm tree in their garden, drinking wine and slivovitz, and often losing the darts in sweet-scented, dry-leaved bushes. The moon would come up, music from a hotel's open-air dance-floor thumped in the background, we laughed a lot – but I began to dread these evenings. It was so obvious that they were spoilt for Didi as soon as I turned up that I used to hesitate in my bedroom, where I had been changing out of my beach clothes, wondering if I should pretend to have letters to write. Then I would hear a particularly merry burst of laughter from the garden, and would say to myself 'Oh what nonsense! Why should I let the little bastard spoil anything for me?' and I would go down. But the bilious looks he gave me, and his instant withdrawal to the fringe of the company, were impossible to ignore.

He lived chiefly on bread, salami and cheese. He had decided that the food was not only disagreeable but made him ill. When he ate with the rest of us he would toy in a martyred way with a dish of pasta, giving sidelong looks of distaste at whatever was on our plates. He contrived to make himself sick once or twice – the food had been 'off', he said, although it had made no one else ill – and since he couldn't drink slivovitz and was determined to find the harmless local wine repulsive, he was condemned to 'horse piss', as he called the light, lager-type Yugoslav beer. If he was punishing me, he was also punishing himself.

Months later he was to claim that he had controlled himself well enough to disguise his evil mood, and particularly what he was feeling towards me; in fact he made it apparent with every flinching withdrawal, every rude contradiction, every turning-away of his eyes, so that the child was the only person who appeared to remain unaware of it.

I remembered a passage in his diary which he had shown me as an example of what happened to him when he was 'in a dep' – his name for his crises. He had taken Gudrun to a beach, and while he was lying on the sand she had picked up a handful of it and had trickled it on to his foot, and even this indirect touch had made him go rigid with disgust and nausea so that a few minutes later he had made the excuse that he must buy cigarettes and had left her, not returning for an hour. Gudrun had been in love with him, and later they had become lovers, so there must have been some physical tension between them which, I was sure, there wasn't between him and me; yet clearly I had become the object of the same kind of revulsion.

If we had been alone together it would have been intolerable. As it was, I had no difficulty in salvaging the best part of my holiday by keeping away from him, and by wondering and laughing about him with my cousin. We knew that we ought to be feeling only pity and concern, but he often cut a comic figure and my cousin and I encourage each other's sense of the absurd. I have sometimes been shocked by a neurotic person's family, when instead of keeping the victim's illness clear in their minds they have spoken of him, or treated him, as though he were a 'normal' person being bloody-minded and therefore blameworthy. Now I know how difficult it would be for them to behave otherwise. It is impossible to remain unhurt, for example, when you are seen as repulsive and heard as idiotic although you are being, as far as you know, just like you always are, even when you are sure that the person seeing and hearing you is doing so through the distorting element of sickness. Or it was, at any rate, impossible for me.

Then one evening Didi surprised me by knocking on my door – his efforts to pass it unheard had until then been creakingly obvious – and suggesting that he and I should dine together at a restaurant outside the town which he had discovered on one of his drives. A peace move! I thought, and accepted with delight.

'It's time we had a talk,' he said while we were having our aperitif. 'We haven't been talking much lately.'

'How could we, when you've been being so beastly?' It was a relief to say it.

'I know – I know. I'm sorry, but I'm having a difficult time, a funny mood.'

'What's wrong?'

He began by admitting his disappointment in the place; it was silly of him, he knew, but the contrast between this little town and what 'the Mediterranean' meant to him made him sad. And besides, he had other troubles … it would be a good thing to talk and bring it all out.

'What are these troubles?'

But at that he became absorbed in the menu, and through most of the meal he continued to be so evasive that I began to feel uneasily that whatever the cause of the tension we were not, after all, going to get down to it. His expression was still the one of fixed and haughty melancholy which he had worn for most of the time since we had arrived in this place, and he hadn't looked at my face once since the evening began. I felt I might blunder if I forced him to the point before he was ready, so we talked only of the people round us and the small-change of our holiday affairs.

It was not until we were drinking our coffee that he said: 'There's something else which has been making me unhappy. It's not easy to say it but I must, for your sake as well as mine.'

'What is it? Go on, whatever it is it can't be so bad as all that.'

'Well ... you've changed since you've been here.'

'In what way, changed?'

'You know that I love you – that I wouldn't be able to say things like this unless I was your friend ...'; and then, in great detail, he let me have it. I was no longer capable, it seemed, of behaving naturally. My manner, my smile, my way of speaking, had all become so affected that they were unbearably irritating and were driving him mad. The way I insisted that everything was 'lovely' just because it was abroad, the way I smiled at people and said 'good morning' to them, the way I found some dreary village 'interesting', some dusty figs 'delicious'. 'Don't you realize', he said, 'that you are making yourself a *figure of fun*? People are laughing at you – they are trying to hide their smiles as you go down the street, and I hate to see people laughing at you because I'm so fond of you.'

Fortunately for my vanity he overstated his case. The grotesque picture of a silly old English spinster abroad which he'd drawn before he was through ought to have been completed with a green-lined parasol and plimsolls (and I was to find in his diary 'she walks by the sea with stockingless legs and *tennis shoes*' – things which I hadn't owned since I left school!). There was some truth in it. I was an Englishwoman of forty-eight with a fair skin which has the inelegant tendency to go red before it goes brown; I was certainly not trying to dress smartly in this unpretentious little seaside town; I was being interested in and pleased by things which were, in their own context, common-place, and enjoyed expressing my interest and pleasure. No one could have hesitated for a moment in placing me as a middle-aged English tourist, and that is not a glamorous thing to be. But Didi exaggerated this picture to such a point that I could at once be safely sure that it wasn't wholly true: I winced, but no blood was drawn.

I fought back by disguising the fact that I had even winced.

'But Didi,' I said, laughing, 'hasn't it occurred to you that if I seem like a silly old Englishwoman abroad it's because that's what I *am*? I know I go on about lovely views and so on, and you don't think they are lovely – but I *do*, so why shouldn't I go on about them if I feel like it? And why shouldn't I smile at people and say good morning, when the people here are so friendly? It may embarrass you – it obviously does embarrass you, and I'm sorry about that – but it's not unnatural or affected, it's just me being how I am.'

This disconcerted him, as I had intended, and he laughed and shrugged.

'You and I, after all, are completely different,' I went on, hoping to steer us away from sparring into discussion. 'The English are so bottled up in their little island that they can't help finding different kinds of places exotic and exciting, and my generation particularly, which didn't get a chance to travel because of the war ...'

He answered vaguely, plainly not interested, and just before we left, while we were waiting for our change, he said without any particular emphasis: 'It's a pity we could never have an affair – a great pity that an affair is impossible between us.'

I looked at him in surprise, assuming that he was referring back to the time when I had wanted him and wondering what had made him think of it now. It was no secret between us that I *had* wanted him. I had several times referred to it in letters when he was pouring out his self-disgust, saying that it was absurd for him to consider himself an unlovable person when he could inspire love so easily – look how strict I had had to be with myself in order to cure myself of being in love with him. I had thought it might bolster his self-esteem to remember it. At this moment, however, the subject was so distant from us in time, and so remote from the mood of hostility in which we were bogged down, that I was puzzled. Perhaps, I thought, he'd brought it up to comfort me by showing that however disagreeable he felt at present, he had not forgotten how close we were; and that was how I decided to take it.

'It *was* a pity,' I said. 'It would have been lovely at the time. But now I know you better I'm thankful it never happened, because if it had we certainly wouldn't still be friends.'

Didi didn't appear to be listening. He was staring past me with hooded eyes and an odd, not at all happy, smile on his lips.

Walking down the steps from the restaurant to the car I realized that the dinner had done nothing to ease our situation, and when he backed the car into another which was parked behind it I was alarmed. He was an extraordinarily good driver and his car was his most treasured possession; normally he handled it impeccably, and for him to reverse violently without looking behind him was a sure indication that he was distraught.

We drove in silence, and I went over the evening in my mind, half angry and half amused at his attack on me, and depressed that disagreeable though it had been, it had obviously not been disagreeable enough to represent the bursting of the boil. And how very odd, I thought, his referring back to that time when I wanted us to have an affair ... and suddenly, as though there had been a flash of light in my head, I gave a silent screech: 'Oh my god – he meant *now*!' He was imagining that I was in love with him again, was yearning for him: he had been *turning me down*!

Oh no! No, he couldn't be imagining that, not at this particular time. Should I ask him? But at that thought my uncertainty vanished: he was imagining just that, I knew for sure. (His diary was to confirm this.) The whole object of the evening had been to show me that I mustn't nurse amorous longings for him because I was a pathetic old spinster in whom they were indecent. It puzzles me now that after that brief time lag I was able to interpret his fantasy so exactly, from so few words. When he recorded the incident he made himself far more explicit than he was in fact. But he might just as well have been explicit, because so powerfully was he projecting his mood, and so acutely were we tuned to each other by the tension between us, that the message now came across as clearly as though he had.

I sat in the car quivering with a mixture of feelings. The first was simple: fury that he should be imagining that I was in love with him. Then came incredulity: how had he done it, at a time when I could hardly control the impatience and annoyance he was inspiring every day? Then fury and incredulity were broken up in inward laughter: poor Didi, oh poor little Didi, the absurdities of his sad, mad mind! And at the same time there was genuine dismay as the purpose of his fantasy became clear. He had brewed it up in order to hurt and to humiliate me as much as he was able. It was frightening to realize that Didi was in a condition to do that.

I must keep silent. He was not in a state to admit reason, and anything I said would be interpreted as poor Diana trying to save her face. I said nothing more but goodnight, and could hardly wait until next morning when I could let off steam by describing the incident to my cousin.

I had another safety valve in being able to tell it all to Luke in my letters (by the following spring Luke had become, willy nilly, an authority on Didi), whereas Didi had only his self-torturing communings with his diary. By the end of our three weeks in Yugoslavia he was deep in his morass, although curiously – perhaps because this crisis lacked the ritual love affair as a launching pad – he didn't seem to recognize it. He knew that he was being irrational and nasty, but he didn't label it 'a dep'.

In spite of being able to stand back from the situation in conversations and letters, and to express to other people the anger I was forbidding myself to express to Didi (I forbade myself to express it because I knew that he had no control over what was happening to him) – in spite of this, during our journey home I allowed malice to escape.

'Tomorrow night,' said Didi, 'let's stop at that nice place we stayed in on our way down – the place where Ana and I met the American sergeant.'

'But it was a *dreary* place,' I said – and so it was: a straggle of houses on the main road in dull country, where we had pulled up only because the end of the day had come and I'd had a headache and hadn't wanted to drive further in search of something better. 'And besides,' I added, looking at the map, 'it would be a very short drive. We'd get there at about four o'clock, and that would mean a huge drive next day if we are going to make Ostende.'

Both these statements were true, and there was no malice in my mind at that stage.

'Ana and I had fun there,' said Didi. 'Don't you remember – no, of course, you went to bed early. But that sergeant was nice, and he invited us to a party in his mess if we came by on our way home.'

'Oh all right, then,' I said. But there had been in Didi's manner that almost imperceptible nuance of over-casualness which I had learnt to interpret as an indication that he was lying. 'I wonder what he's up to?' I thought when I was in my bedroom.

I remembered the inn he was talking about. It had been uninteresting but comfortable. We had eaten in the bar ... and suddenly I remembered the landlady, who had served us: a pretty woman, dark, with a thin face, wearing black. And yes – next morning Didi had said: 'Wasn't she an extraordinary woman to come across in a German pub? She spoke marvellous French, you know, and she told Ana and me she was brought up in the Middle East.' That was it, of course: the landlady in the pub was 'elegant'! Didi was planning to lay her.

And why shouldn't he? He had been having a horrible time and he deserved a treat. But the deviousness of his approach suddenly seemed acutely annoying. His usual pattern was to be secretive about some of his affairs and open about others – they divided at about fifty-fifty, according to no rule that I could see – so there was nothing surprising in his being secretive about this one. It was just that I chose to be irritated that this time he'd favoured secrecy. Besides, it really would be boring for Ana and me to have to kill an afternoon in that dull place – 'The only place we've been through on the whole trip,' I said to myself, 'which is as dull as Rickmansworth!'

At breakfast next morning I took out the map again and found a stopping-place which made better sense. 'This was a pretty place,' I said. 'I remember thinking how charming it looked, and it's nearly a hundred miles further on than the other. It would divide up the distance much better.'

Didi was staring out of the window with a distrait expression. 'Oh well,' he said, 'we'll see how it goes. We'll see how long the drive takes.'

Throughout our journey he had been the one who was, rightly, insistent on early starts. This morning he dawdled. He lingered over his coffee, moved in slow-motion, forgot things, said he must go out for cigarettes before we started.

'We can get them as we drive through the village,' I said. 'It's getting very late.'

Not once did I allow myself a word that was not warranted by the situation; he couldn't *prove* that I was needling him. The road was good, and Didi was driving steadily at thirty-five miles an hour. 'Is the car not pulling well today?' I asked innocently. Before we had been driving an hour he suggested that we should stop for coffee. 'I don't really want any yet,' I said. 'Do you, Ana?' Later we stopped in the outskirts of a big city to change a cheque. 'Why don't we go for a little walk?' said Didi, and I said, 'What, *here*? Are you mad!' That time the vista of tramways, tenement buildings, supermarkets and waste lots was so comically far from tempting to a walk that it was all I could do not to give the game away openly and say '*Really*, Didi, you must do better than that!'

In the whole drive I made perhaps two other such remarks, both of them as reasonable; but Didi knew why he was driving so slowly and suggesting coffees and walks, so not for one moment did he stop feeling the needle in his skin. I worked hard at concealing my grin, but no doubt my expression betrayed as much as his did, and anyway we were still unnaturally tuned to each other. As I had been certain of what he was up to on our drive back from that restaurant in Yugoslavia, so he was certain of what I was up to now.

The place looked even duller in the afternoon than it had at night. We reached it at three forty-five, for all his dawdling, and as we entered it poor Didi felt compelled to say, in a strangled voice, 'If you *really* don't want to stay here we'll go on, of course.' – 'Nonsense,' I said lightly. '*I* don't mind. You want to stay here, so why shouldn't we. You're the one who is driving, after all.' It occurred to me that this was exactly the exchange of a married couple pretending not to be quarrelling. And as with a married couple, ritual restraint heralded outburst. While we were unpacking the car Didi said, with an attempt at normalcy, 'What are you going to do now?'

'Wash my hair,' I snapped with a viciousness in my voice which astonished me. 'What the hell else is there to do in this bloody place?'

Up in my room I tried to be genuinely glad of this chance to wash my hair, but bad temper wrestled with shame, and the water was cold. I lay on my bed reading a novel which I had earlier decided was too trivial to finish. I would go down at seven o'clock, and see how Didi was doing in his campaign on the landlady. It had better be successful after all this absurd carry-on.

When I went down Didi and Ana were standing at the bar drinking schnapps – he must have had a good many by then – the landlady was talking to them, and there was a man sitting to one side with a ledger in front of him.

'Ah, here you are,' said Didi. 'What will you have? You remember our landlady – and this', he added in a carefully colourless voice, 'is our landlord, who was away the last time we were here.'

The French *pouffer dans son mouchoir* is more expressive than the English 'stifle one's laughter'. *J'ai pouffé dans mon mouchoir*. I struggled to hide it, but whatever the resulting expression, Didi could read it. He had read it in advance, for that matter, the moment he himself had been introduced to the husband. Quickly, quickly, I thought, I must talk of something, talk about anything … and I can't remember what I said. All I can remember is Didi's suddenly turning on me and shouting at the top of his voice: 'You don't know anything about it! SHUT UP!'

There was silence in the bar. Ana stared into her glass, the landlady, who understood English, raised her eyebrows, and the landlord looked up, startled.

The forms for registration were lying on the bar. I picked one up, said to Ana 'I think I'll fill this in now,' and went over to a table on the far side of the room. How were we going to eat? I was wondering. How could we sit down to the same table – but to insist on being served separately would look too absurd.

A few minutes later this problem was solved by the entrance of the American sergeant whom Didi and Ana had met when we were last there. He greeted them warmly, took in my presence, said 'So your friend is here tonight, why don't you all join me for dinner,' and herded them over to where I was sitting.

Clearly the pub didn't often have visitors so exotic as an Egyptian man travelling with a Yugoslav girl and an English-woman, and the sergeant, who had a room there, considered us entertainment for the evening. He was a friendly man and under his influence we got on well enough for about half an hour, until he reverted to a conversation he'd had with Didi when they first met.

'So you're a Communist,' he said. 'You know something? I don't believe it. I don't believe you're any more of a Communist than I am.'

Ana and I spoke simultaneously, she to say 'Of course he isn't, he knows nothing about it,' and I to say 'How did you size him up so quickly?' It was on me that Didi turned.

'How dare you!' he screamed – people who had come in and were standing at the bar swivelled round in astonishment. 'How dare you say anything about Communism! You're ignorant, it's all hypocrisy with you – being left-wing, being progressive, a lot of shit ... Look,' he screamed at the sergeant, 'there are these people in England, they live in a part of London called Hampstead where she lives and they think they're left-wing because it's the smart thing to be, but it's nothing but fashion with them, nothing but fashion, they've no knowledge, no feeling, no passion – don't take any notice of the silly bitch, she doesn't know what she's talking about.'

The grounds he had hit on for attack were too mad, I couldn't retaliate. I hadn't been talking about Communism, and I have never pretended to any political position. I have even stated clearly in a book which I supposed Didi to have read, even if he didn't like it, my own feeling of guilt at never having been politically engaged. I stared at Didi, dumbfounded, and saw pure hatred staring back at me.

I was aware of the sergeant's astonishment and of the gaping people at the bar. The hatred in Didi's eyes called up an instant desire to strike back as viciously as possible and I was trembling with rage, but I couldn't embark on a screaming match in front of these strangers. Instead I got to my feet and said, my voice shaking, 'I'm going upstairs' – then, to the sergeant: 'The trouble with us is that we've been cooped up in the same car too long.'

'No, no,' said Didi, jumping up. 'You stay, Ana and I will go out,' and he hustled her away.

'Yes, you sit down,' said the sergeant. 'Have another drink. Looks like your friend is quite an excitable guy.'

I took some deep breaths, gulped a schnapps, and managed (to my own surprise) to spend quite an agreeable further half-hour with the sergeant before going to my room. I knew that what I should do was part with Didi at once. He couldn't be more than a long day's drive from Düsseldorf, where he had friends; it would be far better to leave him here in Germany rather than have to send him back later.

But when I counted what was left of my money my heart sank. I would have to give Didi enough for his petrol, and Ana and I would have to get ourselves to wherever we could pick up a train for Ostende, pay for rail tickets – and then, would our tickets as passengers on a car ferry be valid for an ordinary boat? I didn't think so. We had only just enough money on us for the journey as we were making it, and were going to arrive home with only a shilling or two left, so any extra expense was impossible. I was stuck with Didi.

The next day's drive was silent. I chose to sit in the back all the way, and we had to concentrate so hard on covering too great a distance in too short a time that lack of talk seemed natural. Twelve hours to Ostende, then the crossing, then the night drive from Dover to London during which we ran into thick fog: it was a gruelling day, but at least it allowed me to feel genuine admiration and gratitude for the way Didi drove. Not once in that long day did he gamble on his quick reflexes, but became instead more careful the more tired he was. Home at last, we were all too fatigued for more than 'Goodnight'.

5 The Game

So that winter's crisis began, the crisis called 'Diana' – for that's what it turned out to be in spite of the lack of the customary love affair.

Although we patched up our quarrel, Didi and I avoided each other as much as possible. This was not difficult, because my spare room now became free and he was able to move into it, but I didn't want to appear to be rejecting him. The more hostile he became, the more evident it was that he was sick and that he needed not punishment but support, so although I steered clear of him for most of the time I tried to make it seem a matter of chance. If, for instance, I had people to dinner whom he liked, and whom earlier I would have asked him to join, it would now seem pointed if I left him out so I didn't do so. If I had roasted a chicken and was unable to finish it because I was going out, I would say as I would have said before, 'There's half a chicken in the fridge, love, do finish it up.' If he was having a drink with my cousin when I dropped in to see her (he liked her more as he liked me less), I would tell the kind of gossip he normally enjoyed as though I expected him still to enjoy it. I wanted him to feel that when his black mood lifted he would find me still there as he used to see me – someone on whom he could depend for affection and security – because it seemed to me that when he turned against people of whom he was fond, as he was doing against me, he was in some way challenging them to go on loving him; and that perhaps if he were able to feel that one of them had at last met the challenge, however far he pushed it, his pattern of hopelessness might break. At this stage it was only by hoping that I might conceivably end by doing him some good that I could continue to endure him.

Meanwhile a friend of mine had offered him a part-time job, to be paid out of petty cash for so long as she could get away with it. It was little more than typing envelopes for a few hours a day, and she could pay him only £5 a week, but I suspected by then that anything more demanding would be beyond Didi. The truth was that he had no conception of what a real job of any kind entailed, and that many more people than I knew about must have contributed to his keep in the past. Sometimes he asked me 'What do you *do* all day in your office?' and a description of it which suggested that it might be hard work brought a sceptical look to his face as though he were recognizing a kind of play-acting indulged in by 'grown-up' people: *he* knew, of course, that jobs were simply a method of conning money and status without risk.

He had started occasionally to look at 'Situations Vacant' columns, and two or three times he applied for something and I wrote him a glowing reference. I did it with no hesitation, but with a twinge of guilt. I had to tell myself repeatedly that he *could* do this particular job if he wanted to, that it was true that (if he liked his colleagues – no, forget that) – true that he would be agreeable and amusing to work with, and might well have bright ideas. And he had, after all, stuck the Pay Corps for about eighteen months ... Supposing there was someone in this office who took to him at once (and that could easily happen), so that the display of competence and energy which he put up to start with was confirmed by an audience and he began to take real pleasure in it, wasn't it possible that he might become genuinely involved in his work? Surely it must be, so the chance mustn't be missed. But secretly I was almost relieved when each time the troublesome business of applying for a labour permit made them decide on someone else. By far the most likely result of Didi's getting work, and I knew it, was a whole series of new complications.

For some weeks he had a partiality for advertisements for secretaries: 'Editor of progressive new magazine needs secretary with initiative and a sense of humour', and so on.

'But Didi, he wants a *girl*,' I would say. 'A girl who is trained as a shorthand-typist.'

'How do you know? It doesn't say so.' (Anything I said was suspect.)

'I know because that's what "secretary" means.'

'It doesn't always.'

He had lived in Europe for a long time and many of his girl-friends must have worked in offices, but he was choosing to see a secretary as an urbane young man in an impeccable suit hovering at the elbow of some potentate: the *homme de confidence*, the one who deals with tiresome mistresses and through whom people seeking favours attempt to approach his employer.

I came across one real job within his range: assistant in a bookshop. It was a new shop and the salary was only £10 a week to start with, but £10 a week was £10 more than Didi had, and he loved books, could charm anyone he chose to charm and was quick with figures: he would have made a good assistant in a bookshop. I hurried home to tell him about it, thinking that surely this was news good enough to cheer him up.

'How much do they pay?' he asked, his voice suspicious.

'£10 a week.'

'An eight-hour day for *that*! Are you mad? It's not worth my while to go and see him.'

I was so angry that I was speechless, and I was baffled too. Surely there was one un-neurotic element in his depression: his humiliation at depending on me for his roof and food, and on my cousin (as he had started to do at that time) for pocket-money? Surely he was genuinely longing to be rid of this? I had not yet realized how much the hungry maw of his illness demanded humiliation (agonizingly sensitive to it though he felt himself to be), and that the one kind of job he would always shy away from was the 'real' one he was capable of doing.

The little job offered by my friend wasn't 'real'. He could see it half as a joke and half as generosity on his part in helping her out, besides which she was an amusing woman whose company he enjoyed. Typing envelopes was a bore, but spending several hours a day with Sheila was a pleasure. He started cheerfully, as he had started the stairs and the plans for our holiday, insisting on reorganizing her filing system for her; and by the time he gave up, leaving it half done and in a state of chaos, she had become another of those people so concerned for him that they put up with his ways. From the point of view of the job, she told me later, she was thankful when her accountant began to ask awkward questions and she had to tell Didi that she could no longer employ him, but she missed him badly. Even when he was 'in a dep', Didi enjoying someone and wishing to please them exercised a charm which was far more than a superficial or deliberate trick.

Another hopeful event on the material level was that he was commissioned to write a children's book for which he would get £75 on signature of the contract and another £75 when he delivered the book. He wrote the first half quickly, and it was excellent; but the publisher was slow in sending him the first cheque, failed to answer his letters and dodged his telephone calls. It was carelessness and inefficiency, not villainy, but I couldn't convince Didi of this, and by the time the cheque arrived he was determined to 'have no more to do with those crooks'. I tried to smother my certainty that although the writing had come to him pleasantly and easily, and the second £75 would have been as welcome as the first (which had vanished overnight), the book would never be finished.

I tried to be optimistic because I needed optimism. If I could believe that Didi's morale might gradually be built up by going to an office every day and by getting back to his typewriter, I could believe that he might become a happy presence again – and even that one day he might be able to pay rent for his room. I had recently made some extra money from my writing, so at present the rent wasn't crucial to me, but it would become important again. A happy and independent Didi would be the lodger of my choice, so I went on hoping for him.

But Didi was unable, even if we saw nothing of each other for as much as six or seven days at a time, to forget the irritation I was causing him, and every now and then he would be compelled to scratch the itch. He would have a few drinks, bringing himself up to the point where he experienced an illusion of mellowness, and would knock at my door with apparent amiability to offer me his car for shopping or something of the kind. I would be pleased. I never learnt not to respond to these peace moves, partly because I was so much hoping for peace, and partly – I think – because at the moment when they were made they were genuine as far as Didi consciously knew. I would greet him warmly, offer him a drink, ask him for news of Sheila, or how the children's book was going.

Didi would answer my questions (shrugging off the subject of the book) and would then begin to wander about the room in an elaborately nonchalant way, using his hands a lot as he spoke: slow, graceful gestures as though he were manipulating words which floated invisibly in the air around him. He would smile often – an irritatingly 'knowing' smile – but he would avoid looking at me, and sooner or later he would launch on what I came to call 'the home-truth game': the game he had started in the restaurant in Yugoslavia.

'Sweetheart Diana,' he would say (he was always lavish with endearments, so it took me a little while to see that on these occasions he was extra-lavish); 'Sweetheart Diana, I am going to say something rather horrible.'

'Oh dear, must you?'

'Perhaps I oughtn't to say it, sweetie, but I only do it because I love you. What's the point of being friends if we can't say the truth? Normally I'd keep my mouth shut, but now I'm a little drunk so I'm able to say it, and I'm going to take the chance. You know how I love you, you know how grateful I am to you – I don't have to tell you that. ['Here it comes!' I'd think.] You're a very good person, a generous person, but I can't help seeing that you've got one fault which spoils it all. You are a terrible hypocrite.'

'In what way?'

'I think you probably can't help it, love, it's in your nature. You're not *capable* of genuine feeling – except with Luke, of course [he never risked a dig of any sort connected with Luke

87

because he knew it was too dangerous]. I'm beginning to notice it more and more, and it makes me sad because it's so sad for you. None of your relationships are sincere, not even with your cousin, or with X or Y [mentioning my two oldest friends]. It's a pity, because it spoils your goodness.'

Anger would have started churning in me at once – even if every word he said was true, what damnable impertinence to say it! – but if he was playing this game, so was I, and I scored by not letting him see when he hurt or angered me. Clamping down on my rage (and simultaneously realizing that in clamping down I was, indeed, being hypocritical), I would neatly take the wind out of his sails by asking: 'But if it's in my nature, what can I do about it?'

He would always avoid such questions, waving his hands, smiling – his smile intolerably smug – and staring over my shoulder.

'What ought I to do about it?' I'd insist. 'If I'm a hypocrite I'm sorry. I don't want to be, and my feelings feel genuine to me.'

He would side-step: 'It's cruel of me to have said it, I know. It must hurt you . . .'

'No, it doesn't hurt me, but . . .'

'I expect it's just my horrible supersensitiveness, and I ought to shut up. I've no right to say such things to you.'

'You haven't really, have you?' – and at that he would look stricken and would go quickly and silently out of the room.

I always won these games because I held all the trumps. If it were to become an *exchange* of home truths, it was I who commanded the murderous ones. It was I who could have said: 'Hypocrite? What about you, swallowing your bile so that you can continue living for free in this flat – continue to be nothing more than a parasite? What about you, saying you "love" me when your every word and gesture since we were in Yugoslavia makes it clear that I irritate you to distraction? Who are you to accuse me of anything?'

But my victory could never be conclusive because of the very strength of my hand. All I needed to do was show a corner of a card – 'You haven't really, have you?' – and he was in retreat, going out to get even drunker, or retiring to his room to lie on his bed in the dark. What would have happened to him if I had slammed down my whole hand? I was certain that he would be destroyed.

This sense of the destructive power of my own anger if I unleashed it may have come partly from my upbringing, the emphasis put on self-control in a middle-class English family of my period. A child forbidden to express rage freely is said to develop a neurotic fear of its own dark powers. But although my family aimed at self-control – it was high among the virtues we were told we must acquire – it was better at theory than practice. If I had become inhibited in expressing anger, what I had learnt about the emotion from my parents' quarrels or the occasions on which my nails met in my brother's flesh must have had as much to do with the inhibition as the precepts by which I was raised. The stronger restraint came, I believe, from the truth about Didi. Even when I was reacting on the surface as though towards a normal adult who happened to be behaving disagreeably, I never lost the sense that I was really faced with the terrible vulnerability of 'a child of seven or eight' masquerading as a man.

I was not calm after these encounters. I would shake with anger and be condemned to hours of inward muttering: 'The little bastard – how dare he! – Yugoslavia – the stairs, the job he wouldn't even try for, the paint on my carpets, the book he isn't finishing, the money he's started borrowing from people who have almost none, the money he's costing me [when I reached this one I became even angrier, so much did I detest catching myself at it], his boozing, the glass he broke last week without even saying he was sorry': the whole list of his sins and inadequacies, large and small, would unreel through my head – and at the same time I would be smarting ('Damn him, damn him!') because it was rare for Didi's 'home truths' to have no truth in them.

If he led with hypocrisy – well, how could I persuade myself that he was wrong? I knew exactly what he meant. When I say I love my friends I am not insincere, but I am one of those people who are hardly ever totally involved in an emotion. There is almost always a 'watcher' in the back of my mind, and a pretty beady-eyed watcher at that. To Didi, who experienced emotions as blinding waves filling every corner of his being, how could this opposite kind of nature seem anything but artificial and cold? It *is* cold. It is all very well to abhor self-deception, to be more interested in how things are than in how they ought to be, to be capable of acting against an impulse because the impulse seems wrong or foolish, but it entails a lack of responsiveness to people and situations of which one cannot be proud.

And certainly the cold and beady eye was fixed on Didi, and on myself in relation to him. Continuing to behave – or trying to behave – as though it wasn't, and as though the affection which I thought he needed was the only motive of my behaviour: what was that, if not hypocrisy? Damn him, damn him, damn him!

Didi could often draw blood of this kind, and I never felt free to stab back. I knew so well how even the mildest reproof ('Oh Didi, *why* can you never remember to put the hammer back in the drawer?') could keep him huddled in his room for an hour, certain that no one could ever stand him, so how could I possibly bring down on him the punishment he was asking for? It had never occurred to me before that the position of strength can be a weak one.

No, I didn't really win these games. We tied. He failed to achieve what he was driving for – getting me to scream at him, to flay him, to annihilate him. And I failed to achieve what I was driving for – annihilating him on my own terms, not his. I came nearest to winning on the one occasion when it seemed that he had won.

A dear friend of mine had been very ill and was passing through London after a serious operation. She was staying with another friend who gave a dinner party for her, and we knew her well enough to realize that this must be a gay party with no evident concessions made to her illness: her sense of style would make anything but gaiety intolerable to her. I was asked to bring Didi to the party.

As I entered the room I saw, with an agonizing shock, that my friend had not, as she insisted, recovered from the operation. As it turned out her condition at that time was misleading and she would live for three more years, but on that evening she looked as though she would be dead within months. I had no doubt of it. I obliterated the impression at once – it made it all the more important that the party should be a happy and natural one – and managed, as everyone else did, not only to 'act' as though the evening were enjoyable, but to enjoy it. Didi fell for my friend and her husband, who really did have the qualities of elegance and style he so loved, and was amusing and charming, we all drank a lot, and the party didn't end till well after midnight.

There was no sense of strain while it was going on. It was only on leaving and getting into Didi's car that I understood I was exhausted. Suddenly all I could think of was my friend's threadlike thinness lost in her dress, and what had happened to her face, and even my bones ached. Didi began to comment on her wit, and I said: 'Yes, she's marvellous – but she's terribly terribly ill, much iller than I was expecting, and I feel so sad that I can hardly bear it. Do you mind, love, if we don't talk.'

He was silent for a few minutes, then began to talk again. Feeling that I ought to try to overcome my grief and fatigue – the situation was, after all, nothing to Didi, who had met her for the first time that evening – I answered briefly, hardly listening, until he said: 'There was one thing which made me very angry – the way you told her I'd painted the stairs. It makes me very angry when you try to give the impression that I'm your lover like that.'

I felt a double incredulity. It was impossible to believe that he could have interpreted my reference to his painting the stairs in that way, and it was impossible to believe that he could be so insensitive to what I was feeling about my friend that he could think me capable of forgetting it in order to spar with him. I said: 'Oh please, Didi, not now. I asked if we could be quiet – I do really want to be.'

He screamed at me: 'You think that because you are in the position of power you can make me do anything you like. I can't stand it, I won't stand it.'

I then did something I have never done before or since in my adult life. I burst into tears. On other occasions, of course, I have wept, but never has a storm of weeping overcome me suddenly and unexpectedly, as it did then. That at this moment, instead of being granted silence and understanding, I had to be goaded by this idiotic and irrelevant egotism – it was impossible to bear.

I didn't even try to stop crying. Huddling away from him, in the corner of my seat, I sobbed wildly all the way home. At one point he said in a subdued screech 'Shut up!' and I gasped back childishly 'Shut up yourself! You aren't even driving the right way.' – 'I *am* driving the right way,' he said furiously (he wasn't), and we were silent again except for my sobbing.

When we got home I ran upstairs and into my room, where I fell on my bed and went on crying. Surprisingly, he came in after me, and after standing awkwardly beside me for a few moments, began to stroke my shoulder. He could offer me no comfort – it was horrible to feel the emptiness there, to know that the person standing by me who I had believed in spite of everything to be a friend, and who still in spite of everything believed himself to be a friend, just *had* nothing to offer in any situation which didn't directly concern himself. 'I'll go and have a bath,' I mumbled, to escape from him. He followed me across the hall, still dabbing at my shoulder, and feeling dimly the extent of his confusion and dismay I managed to say 'Yes, I know you are trying to be kind, you didn't mean it.' Then at last I was alone in the bathroom and was able to recover.

That evening Didi seemed to win by pushing me to the point of collapse, but because what I had collapsed over was to do with another person, not him, he felt it as defeat. I know this because it was the only evening in that period of which he left no record at all in his diary.

It marked a turning point for me. It marked the point where I recognized that I must never – not even when he was 'well' again – expect from Didi what one normally expects from a friend. When he gave anything to other people – as he often did, as he had done earlier to me and was to do again – it was by the happy accident of their chancing to appreciate what he chanced to be 'giving off'. If he happened to be in a mood to charm, to find things amusing, to respond lovingly, to use his intuition (which could be sharp) on people's behaviour, to apply his intelligence, then whoever was around would benefit; but he was so hermetically walled up in himself that he was unable to discover in other people any constant reason to attend to them, still less to be considerate of them, and he couldn't answer their demands. Let them stop reflecting back on him some aspect of himself that at the moment was important to him, and they would become unreal; and if they expected *him* to reflect back some aspect of *them*, they became intolerable, they were asking him to do something he couldn't do, putting a painful strain on him from which he had to escape. I had expected him to understand what I was feeling about my friend's illness, and to sink his self-absorption for a while in order to care about my condition ... and it had been like asking a child to fill in your income-tax returns for you.

Luke wrote: 'If you are *sure* you don't want him there any more, you must kick him out.' If Luke had become an expert on Didi, he was even more an expert on me; other people simply said 'You must kick him out.'

I was not sure. Pleasure had vanished but the sense of responsibility had increased, and there is some kind of satisfaction in indulging a sense of responsibility – a suspect kind, no doubt, in that even if it is harmless it is not simply what it appears to be. Power? Was I enjoying a sense of power over another person? I think not. My inhibition against exercising the power I had in any practical way was absolute, and when I used the advantages of detachment and comparative sanity in order to 'win' our games, I was doing it in self-defence, to prevent the element of truth in Didi's accusations from hurting me too much. What had trapped me, I am almost sure, was my acceptance of the role (my grabbing of the role?) of mother.

I could imagine a scene during which I kicked Didi out, and I could imagine (I often did) enjoying such a scene, but as soon as I had to picture that forlorn little figure puttering away in his car – where to, and with what in his pocket? – my heart contracted with pain. It was as though I were *physically* incapable of causing that loneliness and hopelessness, and would be doing myself a violence if I caused it. If at any time he had enough cash on him to survive for a few weeks, or perhaps get back to Germany, I might be able to tell him to go, but not otherwise. I began to do what he himself did over the £75 which he would get from the publisher if he finished the children's book, and various other sums of money (all of which either proved illusory, or were at once drunk and gambled) which he sometimes announced he might earn from this or that; I began to feel that if we *named* them firmly enough they were as good as real. 'When I get paid for that translation I'm going to do ...'; 'When I do that talk for the BBC ...'; of course I knew by now that this was only talk, but by making an act of faith in it I could keep my spirits up, as he did.

Because Didi himself was loathing the situation even more than I was. There were times when he failed to record something in his diary because it was too shaming – perhaps he even failed to remember it – but every 'borrowing' which would never be repaid, every raid on my whisky or my cousin's, every small lie to cover an evening's gambling, every unjustified rudeness or coldness was recorded with bleak honesty. He was disgusted by these things, disgusted by the irrationality of the loathing he was feeling for me, disgusted and baffled by his own inability to do what thousands of exiles manage to do: earn their keep by buckling down to whatever work their persistence finds, however uncongenial. He wrote about this once, from a deep pit of despair when the only alternative to constant humiliation and guilt that he could envisage was death. How absurd this was, he wrote, when death was *not* the only alternative. He could restore his self-respect any day by finding a job and starting to earn his living; and although working was 'something I absolutely loathe the prospect of', surely even he must admit that it would be less disagreeable than killing himself? If he could see this, he asked himself, why, why, why was he so totally unable to act on it?

94

In spite of his crippling inertia, it was he, not I, who tried to end it. I gave a lunch party for eight people one Sunday, and he was there because he had been particularly hostile in the previous week so that I couldn't exclude him without appearing to be punishing him. It must have been a good party, because at seven o'clock that evening they were still there, several of them – including Didi – very drunk. As there was a good deal of wine still unopened I could see that there was some time to go before it would end. For the first four hours I had enjoyed my guests, but now the drunk ones had slithered into that stage of fatuous argument in which each goes into whatever act he always goes into when drunk, and I became bored. With relief I remembered that a friend had asked me to her house that evening to watch a television programme about President Kennedy's assassination, so at half past seven I looked at the clock, exclaimed with dismay, and said that I must go, thinking that this would break the party up. It didn't. They hardly noticed what I said, or my departure, but the television programme was to last until after midnight, the level in the last demi-john had sunk, so it seemed reasonable to hope that by the time I returned they would be gone.

At about eleven thirty my friend's telephone rang and it was Didi, asking if I'd like a lift home. They had all gone on to a pub, he said, and had a splendid evening. We told him to come and watch the end of the programme, and he was with us in fifteen minutes.

He held drink uncommonly well, so he must have consumed a vast amount to have become noisy and foolish, only a little way from falling about, as he was that night. As soon as he sat down in front of the television screen he began to barrack the speakers, shouting 'Bloody Yanks – hypocritical bastards – boo – down with them!' whenever a member of the Warren Commission appeared. My friend's husband was ill with 'flu in the next room, trying to sleep – the sort of thing about which Didi was normally considerate – but he paid no attention to our attempts to hush him, so as soon as the programme ended I took him away. On the way to the car he went on shouting 'That's what I can't stand about you bloody British, you have no passion, you sit there watching those bastards talking their shit, "listening to both sides", "being fair" – it makes me want to vomit.'

I had drunk a lot myself since lunchtime, and I was sleepy, longing to be at home and in bed. The remains of the drink in me stirred in reaction to his noise and folly, giving me a sharp impulse to smack his face, but the sleepiness won: better to humour him and get him home quickly. But when we were in the car he said: 'How much money have you got on you?'

'About £2, why?'

'Because I haven't any, need I say, and we're going gambling.'

'Oh no we're not. I'll need those £2 tomorrow, and anyway all I want is to be in bed.'

'I didn't really mean we'd gamble – only I'm out of ciggies and the only place I can get Gauloises this time of night is the club.'

'Too bad, you'll have to make do with mine till tomorrow.'

He made no answer and started the car, and a few seconds later I saw we were driving away from home.

'Where are we going?'

'To the club.'

At that moment we were stopped by traffic lights. 'You may be going to the club, but I'm not,' I said, a violent wave of irritation sweeping through me, and I whisked out of the car and began walking fast down a street which I saw with satisfaction was one-way, so that he couldn't follow me. It led towards Regent Street where, no doubt, I would find a taxi sooner or later.

Drunk though he was, Didi noticed the one-way sign and saw how to get round it. He came after me in reverse, bumping the kerb, the car's engine roaring, and flung open the passenger's door saying 'Stop this bloody nonsense, get in.'

I hesitated, but it was after one o'clock on a Sunday night, much colder than I had thought, and so far the glimpse of Regent Street had shown no traffic at all. I knew that I had won in that Didi would now drive home, so I got in.

Glancing sideways without turning my head I could see his

hands trembling on the steering wheel, and he was breathing heavily and slowly, deep shuddering breaths. Twice he took a wrong turning and I almost spoke to prevent his doing so, but it was as though the car were full of explosive gas and a word would have been a spark: I kept silent.

Back in the flat, I found that my own temper had calmed and that I was only wearily annoyed with him for having got so stupidly drunk. Why let the sun go down on my wrath, I thought, and as I was going into my room I said: 'Goodnight – thank you for coming to pick me up.'

'I'm leaving,' he said.

I turned to look at him. His hair was on end, his mouth was trembling, his eyes were so wide that I could see the white above the iris.

'Do you mean *now*?' I said.

'Yes, now. You must understand one thing – you must. I love you with all my heart. But don't try to stop me because I just can't stand one more second of all this.'

All this? I thought. What 'all this'? That I wouldn't give him £2 to gamble with in the middle of the night? Jesus god! Have I got to deal with this now, when all I want is to be in bed? He had sprung it too suddenly for me to feel sure what to say, but I could see that we had moved on to ground where he had to be 'managed'.

What I said was: 'I shan't try to stop you, Didi. You're quite right, we've been getting on each other's nerves too long and it's time you left. But you don't have to go *now*, in the middle of the night. Tomorrow morning would be far better.'

'No, it must be now, it will be too difficult tomorrow. Please don't argue, sweetie, I'll be out of here in an hour.'

'Where will you go?'

'What does that matter?'

'Oh Didi, don't be such a fool. You're stinking drunk, you can hardly drive – why on earth go charging off like this?'

'I must.'

'Look – go to bed now' – I took him by the arm and steered him into his room, pushing him down on to his bed – 'have a bit of sleep, anyway, to sober you up.'

'I'm not drunk.'

'You're stinking drunk – literally stinking, the fumes are horrible. You're in no state to drive and you know it.'

'You mustn't think it's because I don't love you, you mustn't think that.'

This repetition of his love for me almost brought my temper back again. Meaningless idiocy, it sounded, at this moment when his revulsion had finally broken right out; and at the same time the tone of his voice and the way his head had started to loll made me think: 'God, he's reached the maudlin stage, he never does that, he must be very near passing out – he *can't* be allowed to drive now, I must stop him somehow.'

Anger, I thought. Reasoning is useless – bully him.

'Didi!' I said sharply. 'Pull yourself together, you're behaving like an hysterical idiot,' and I grabbed his shoulders – he was sitting on the bed – and shook him. His head waggled.

'Didi!', and I slapped him fairly hard on his left cheek, my hand moved more by the accumulated annoyance of the evening than by the need of the moment.

A smug smile swam to the surface of his decomposed face – it was decomposed in that ugly way which occurs in advanced drunkenness, when the features seem to have lost their relationship to each other.

'It's you who are hysterical,' he said, 'not me.'

I stood and looked at him. He stared straight ahead, still smiling smugly. I realized that I would have to battle with him for hours if I was to prevent his going, and that I didn't want to prevent it.

'All right,' I said. 'If you want to go now, you'd better go. I shall have a bath.'

I said it simply because it had occurred to me that I would now be unable to sleep if I went to bed straight away, but once I was in the bathroom I remembered that his shaving and washing things were there and that he would want to pack them: if I took a long time over my bath he might pass out while waiting for me to finish. I spent over half an hour in the bathroom, but as soon as I was out I heard him crossing the hall to fetch his things. He packed very quickly and quietly, considering how drunk he was, and before another half hour had passed there was the bumping of suitcases on the stairs, the click of the flat door, and then, a minute later, the familiar sound of the little car starting up and tock-tocking off down the street.

I lay awake for a long time. The flat felt empty. How foolish to think I could feel its emptiness – if Didi had been asleep next door the silence would have been no different, I was only imagining its sadness. And tomorrow – or if not tomorrow, the next day – what a relief it would be to know that I was rid of Didi.

The emptiness which had seemed sad did, indeed, soon become a luxury. There was a lightness in having my flat to myself again, in re-arranging the kitchen to my own taste, in leaving the bathroom door open if I felt like it, in breathing the absence of thunder in the air. It was this pleasure in being alone which made me, I thought, postpone plans to let the spare room. I ought to do so soon, because I had been getting into debt to my cousin for the rent, but I would have a few days' – perhaps a few weeks' – holiday first. So I told myself.

But Didi hadn't left his key behind, and on the second day after he left I realized that he was creeping in to wash and shave while I was out at work. He thought he removed all traces of it, but a towel was damp, there was a black hair on the soap. He had not found anywhere else to live.

My cousin reported that he was coming to her for food. Sheila, for whom he was working, reported that he was distilling despair of such strength that her office appeared to have gone dark. Neither to them nor to anyone else did he say what had happened, beyond that he was no longer living in my flat. He didn't *tell* them that he was sleeping in his car and had nothing to eat but what they gave him, and it was his silence which worked on them.

'You should be thankful to be rid of him,' changed to 'You would be silly to take him back, of course – yes, of course that's out of the question, you mustn't do it,' and then to 'He's suffering terribly, poor little creature.' Finally it became 'If you could bear it, don't you think that perhaps you *ought* to take him back?'

What these kind friends were feeling reflected my own

reactions too accurately for me to hold out against them. It was wonderful to be without Didi, but not wonderful enough to obscure the image I had dreaded, the image of Didi alone, hopeless and helpless – and faced with that image I acknowledged that I was making no plans for the room chiefly because I knew he would soon be back in it.

I went through the motions of being sensible. I wrote to him at Sheila's office saying that he had been right, and that it was obviously impossible for us to live together after we had frayed each other's nerves so badly, but that if he had not yet found anywhere else he could, if he liked, come back to the flat while he was looking. He would have, now, to concentrate on finding work which paid him a living wage, and as soon as he found it he must leave and take another room somewhere else; but meanwhile, if he needed a place 'for the next three or four weeks', the room was there. He returned on the day he got my letter, and I knew at once (although I tried not to admit it) that the reservations it contained might not have been written for all the attention he had given them. I knew too, within a very short time, that the explosion had done nothing to relieve the tension between us.

I wasn't acting only out of determination to help Didi if I could. That motive existed, but when I saw it as the only one I was rationalizing. Disagreeable though our situation was, I was as much hooked on it as he was.

This kind of 'hooking' can only seem extraordinary when viewed from outside. The innumerable married couples who live year after year in mutual torture: how puzzling they appear, because surely any amount of trouble (looking for somewhere else to live, making decisions about the children or about money, upsetting families and all the rest of it) would be better than the endless pain and distress some of them cause each other. One can only assume that they are engaged in a deadly but absorbing game without which they would be bored or frightened, and that the pain it inflicts gives each of them a sharper sense of his or her own reality – or perhaps simply something with which to fill emptiness?

The Game

In an amateurish way, with only half our minds on it (compared with married couples), Didi and I had become involved in such a game. If he was obsessed, so was I. The degree to which I was aware of him betrayed it.

I never passed his door on coming in without noticing whether or not a crack of light showed under it, as though his presence or absence made a difference in the orientation of my own mood; I noted the briskness of his tread as he moved about the flat, the way he handled things in the kitchen, whether he was coughing or not, whether he got into bed as soon as he came in, or paced his room. There was a language of faint creaks, thuds or clinks, the opening and shutting of doors, the time spent in the lavatory, the smell left in the bathroom (Cologne? He's out with a girl tonight), by which I was able to interpret his state. Brisk steps, deft movements, a scented bathroom, noises neither unnaturally subdued nor unusually clumsy, and my heart lightened: the pressure was off, he had turned towards some outside activity and was taking a rest from being a thunder cloud. Mouselike creepings contradicted by his aggressively painful cough, and my heart sank: here we go again. Although a heavy sleeper, I doubt whether I missed any of his homecomings. My flat is remarkably soundproof for noises made above floor level, but its floors are bad. A lodger can talk, laugh, type, make love on a creaky bed (provided it's standing on a sound bit of floor) without my hearing, but when he walks about I know it. I would wake with one eye, just enough to register that Didi was home, had gone to the kitchen to eat, had crossed the hall to his room – thump thump, his shoes were off, the creak of the board beside his bed which meant that he was getting into it – yes, he was in bed now, I could go to sleep again. The amount of time I gave to these observations and the interest I took in them were disproportionate – mad – and so was the intensity, whether amused or appalled, with which I brooded over our encounters, analysed his moves and my own in the home-truths game, and fretted at the annoyances he caused me. Although Luke was still away my days were full – my work is demanding, I have good friends, I was writing – yet there I was, making an almost full-time occupation of Didi.

This did not prevent my being taken by surprise when he struck his climactic blow.

About once every six weeks I spent a weekend in the country with my mother, leaving on Friday night and getting back to the flat at about ten fifteen on Sunday evening. My mother takes no Sunday papers, so taking my own to bed with me when I got home, and reading them in lazy comfort, had become a ritual. Didi knew this ritual well. If he was in when I returned he always came out of his room to give me the papers, and if he was going to be out he would leave them in the hall for me, because our wretched 'game' had not prevented the development of the kind of domestic routine which builds up between people living in the same house.

Before I left, on this particular weekend, he checked on the time of my return. When he did this it meant, usually, that he would take advantage of my absence by inviting a woman to the flat (it was only later that he overcame an inhibition against doing this, however discreetly, while I was there), and didn't want me to catch him at it. He was out when I got back – no line of light under his door – but there were no papers in the hall. I looked in my sitting-room and the kitchen, thought 'Bother him, he's forgotten I want them', then knocked at his door, thinking he might be there but had gone early to bed. There was no answer, so I went in and switched on the light.

I was delighted by what I saw. For some time Didi's room had been in a state of incoherent mess which reflected his mood. He was precise and tidy when he was happy, arranging favourite objects in special ways, and taking a pride in his room, but since we had come back from Yugoslavia he had been leaving dirty clothes on the floor, letting papers drift everywhere, and failing to make his bed. Tonight the room was immaculate. He had obviously spent much time over the weekend in giving it a thorough cleaning. The Sunday papers were on the neatly made bed, and his desk was clear except for one notebook, lying open.

My instant reaction was pleasure at how much better he must be feeling to have restored order in this way, and the pleasure was increased by the sight of the notebook. It was the same size and shape as the book in which he had started his story for children, and I thought 'At last he's decided to finish that story! Hurrah!' As l crossed the room to pick up the papers I paused by the desk and looked at the open page to see whether I was right.

The first words I saw – the last on the page – were: 'I haven't had a woman for over five months!!!!! It is unbelievable, but there you are. It is killing me. The frustration is enormous. If only I weren't so particular – so bloody capricious.' It was his diary.

Those words astounded me. It meant that he hadn't had a woman, for all his party-going and late nights, since we'd returned from our holiday. But even more interesting than this revelation was the possibility of discovering what he had felt about bolting from the flat. 'Well,' I thought, 'he's asked for it. He knows our agreement – anything that isn't put away is likely to be read, and here he is absolutely *presenting* it to me'; and I began to turn back the pages to find the record of that incident.

My own name jumped out at me at once. 'My last entry was getting Diana off my chest and with this entry I am off her back (figuratively I am pleased to say. Literally is too repulsive to even think about).'

The blood rushed up into my face and my hands went cold. It was the same shock as that which follows opening an envelope which looks harmless and finding that it contains an obscene anonymous letter: an unreasonable reaction, considering that I was reading the private diary of someone who, as I knew, had been finding me intolerably irritating for several months, but the difference between deducing Didi's feelings from his behaviour and seeing them written down was going to prove surprisingly great.

'My last entry was getting Diana off my chest ... ' I turned quickly to the last entry.

There is no point in lying or being a hypocrite. I have started to detest her. I find her unbearable. Now, I am obviously diseased. Part of this disease, or one of my many diseases if you wish (you – who?) is that my mental reactions are dependent on my physical response to things. For instance I am always talking about love, yet love to me is physical desire pure and simple. This is leading to the fact that my reactions to Diana are sparked by my physical antipathy to Diana. I find it impossible to live in the same flat as someone whose physical body seems to provoke mine to cringe. This has led me to detest everything she does, says, or writes. I am trying hard to understand the monstrosity of my attitude and I can really only explain it by accepting the fact that I am diseased, abnormal, sick ...

I'd be sitting in my room watching a stupid thing on telly and annoyed with myself for not switching it off and working – writing letters, working on the novel or writing my diary. In her sitting-room her typewriter would go tick tick tick tick tick. 'Christ,' I'd tell myself, 'there she is, hammering away at that bloody mediocre muck – dishing out one tedious stupid sentence after another, and thinking – no, *pretending* it is writing.' And this mood would seize me. Then I would remember all she has done and is still doing for me, so I knock on her door. 'Cup-a-tea, luv?' I say. She's so engrossed (pretending) she hardly hears me. Finishes a sentence, looks at me – very much 'unaware of her environment', so taken up she is by her 'art'. 'I'd love a cup, luv.' Afterwards I go back to my room. 'What a bastard I am,' I keep whispering, 'what a bastard I am.'

Didi would be coming in soon. The sensations of shock returned when I realized how sure I was of this, how certain that whether he knew it or not he had left this diary out on purpose for me to read, and was now agog to know whether I had. I must hurry – let me flick back to Yugoslavia.

Since the beginning of the journey Diana started being *collante* – sticky. Terribly tender, forgiving and loving. She will touch me with her finger and my whole being absolutely cringes in revulsion. If someone I find unattractive suddenly gets this consuming crush on me [Crush on him? Good God!] I become a pole of repulsion. I can't stand it, I get the equivalent of *chair de poule* right inside me. I then become terribly unfair, critical and unwillingly nasty. And then there is this suspicion that she often tries to pass me off as her boy-friend, her lover. This angers me very much indeed …

I can't blame myself more than I would blame someone who is allergic to a plant or a smell …

They were sitting down to lunch and no sooner did I sit down than Diana starts her strange chatter, uttered in a peculiar way, being absolutely imbecile. Being 'jolly' in an English way. She raises her head as though in ecstasy, looks at the horizon, smiles maddeningly, and all this with both a running commentary and statements of things done and to be done. 'I think I SHALL have another glass of this delicious wine' – the wine is 'orrible – 'with some soda water to make a spritze.' She always ends a statement with a particular force – 'a spritZA'. 'Didi shall drive us home and have his siesTA.' She then looks at my arm, comments on its tan, and rubs it with her hand, being coy. She is as red as a lobster, and sticky, and to be coy in that state and being in her fifties is to me unbearable [this slight exaggeration of my age – I was forty-eight – made me shudder with rage] …

In the evening I opened my door slowly and tiptoed down to sit with the others. There we are, talking and laughing, when suddenly a loud voice from upstairs shouts 'Didi!'

'Yes,' I say, angry at this terrible imposition.

'What time is it?'

'I don't know,' I say in a terrible rage.

'I'll be down in a minute.'

And she came – she came down …

I don't know what the Yugoslavs make of her – they must be slightly amused by this strange figure among them, this 'jolly good sort' who plays darts with abandon, running back-wards and forwards and screaming and trying to be funny in an *unnatural* way …

It was an extraordinary and frightening experience, these fragments of things I remembered reappearing in distorted form, another 'reality' (and one in which I was grotesque) jangling with my own. I had a clear memory of that lunch when I ordered a spritze. It was an agreeable one until Didi joined us halfway through, and was then only slightly spoilt by his martyred refusal to try the wine. My cousin and I exchanged looks of mock despair behind his back. *Coy?* I had only tried to disregard his mood and behave as I would have done if he had been cheerful, commenting enviously on his tan and comparing it ruefully with my own arm which was still red, not brown. In retrospect I see that my manner of speaking, my voice, my expression were probably betraying the artificiality of this attempt – be *coy*! And that evening when I had called out of my window to ask what time it was: of course I knew by then that he saw my joining the party in the garden as spoiling it, but 'this terrible imposition' ... 'And she came – she came down', as though I had done something outrageous ... It was monstrous to see myself so reflected.

A greater shock was to come when I reached the entry (written after we were back in London) in which he described our dinner together in the restaurant he had found.

I had taken a date with B [my cousin] for supper together that evening. I was looking forward to that. First, as usual, because she is always well dressed, elegant and beautiful, so I am proud to go out with her. And then she is shy, and I am not embarrassed to be with her, whereas with Diana, particularly in a foreign country, she is apt to be very loud, very jolly, and it embarrasses me. Anyway, I asked Diana if she was hungry and she said no. That day, looking forward to the supper with B, I had cruised the district for the nicest restaurant and had found it. So, Diana having said she wasn't hungry, I told her that I was going out with B. To which she very nonchalantly said 'I shall come too.' I had a feeling, absolutely *not* based on fact, but a feeling nevertheless, that since Diana was paying for my holiday she allowed herself to disregard what I wanted or felt like doing. As I say, this is not true, but it was this sudden feeling which angered.

But this was not all. She drank a wine, went upstairs to B, returned at once and said 'B won't come, we shall go together.' Well, the terrible temper rose at once, of course. It was controlled, but it was boiling without an outlet. Unconsciously she started to irritate me to shouting point. I say unconsciously because poor Diana has no inkling of what goes on in me at times and how the most innocent remark is apt, mysteriously, to infuriate me. I am writing in retrospect, months later, when I think I know her as she really is, and not as how I thought she was. It took this holiday to make me know her (and her me, of course).

So there we were. I said, since she was not hungry, we'd just go and have a quick snack. 'No,' she said, 'let's go where you were taking B. I am hungry now.' She held my hand and caressed my arm as we went up the steps to the restaurant. Earlier, in front of the Yugoslavs, she again insinuated we were lovers, things like 'Didi and I, when we are in London' or 'It's nice living with Didi because he's such a good cook.' Because of my fastidiousness and terrible sensitivity I was irritated.

Now at the restaurant I couldn't stand it any longer. What I told her was simple and brief. But it was enough to change our relationship at once. 'Diana,' I told her, 'I don't want you to make a fool of yourself. You must not get emotionally involved with me. It would be nice if we could have an affair, but we can't, and it shall never happen.' She must have wriggled with pain, but didn't show it. That was all. I gave her a kiss later, but she must have been very humiliated, and understandably so.

This was horrifying because while in all the other entries I recognized the actual happenings, however disconcerting Didi's interpretation of them, in this one I couldn't. The preliminaries to his suggestion that we should dine alone together, so important to him, had vanished from my mind. All I could be sure of – absolutely sure – was my own *surprise* and the words 'A peace move!' which had come to my mind, from which I could also be sure that I did not, in fact, force myself on him in the way he described. In his room that night, skimming quickly, listening for his steps on the stairs, all I could think was 'But it's

not true! He's mad – he's quite mad!', but later my own failure
of memory was to worry me: how much had I, too, been distorting events in favour of my own interpretation? Something of
what he described must have gone on, and I have since con-
structed (not remembered) it in such a way that it could meet
both his recollection of it and mine; but such a construction is
valueless, and I have to leave it that Didi remembered it his
way, and I as I have described it earlier, with the modification
that I could have experienced that sensation of surprise from
his appearing to wish to dine with me in spite of my cousin's
decision not to come, and not from his inviting me out of the
blue.

At the time, while I was reading, there was no room for such
speculation. There was only shock at what seemed to be a
fantasy version of what I was sure had happened. It was only
madness that I was seeing, and I went on seeing it.

A few pages later the word 'Esplanade' caught my eye and
puzzled me. 'In Zagreb we stayed at the Esplanade, a very
luxurious hotel, exactly what I had always imagined Central
European elegance to be.' In Zagreb, we stayed in the Intercontinental. Didi went into raptures over the 'Central European elegance' of the bar and I agreed, saying that it was sensible of the Americans not to have modernized it, at which he
snubbed me fiercely. How could Americans possibly run a
hotel in a Communist country – and even if they could 'the
bloody Yanks' would never have the good taste to leave it like
this. So I went up to my room and fetched the Intercontinental
leaflet, with its New York address, from the drawer in the desk,
and sulkily Didi accepted the truth. Later I would find it funny
and pathetic that he could reject it again so quickly in favour of
the hotel of his imagination, but while I read I could only repeat
'Christ, but he's mad – he really is!'

There was much more, including a fantasy of my stealing
and hiding the keys of his car, which he had lost near the beginning of his stay with me. He had recently come across them in a
drawer in my sitting-room, and had wiped out of his mind the
fact that this was the drawer I had emptied for him when he was
sleeping in that room, as he was doing when the keys were lost.

When he had moved into the spare room I had refilled the drawer with the odds and ends of old material and a bundle of papers which I usually stored there, and hadn't seen the keys, which had – I suppose – slipped under the crumpled lining paper. Now he had been digging about in that drawer (and why, when it again contained my things?), and as soon as he saw the keys became convinced that I had hidden them there. They locked the steering of the car, and it had been a tedious and expensive business getting a locksmith to it (I paid!) – and I, he was sure, had been gloating in mysterious malice through it all. He had the grace to express himself puzzled at my behaviour, but his puzzlement made his certainty of it all the more alarming because all the madder.

There were also times when, he was sure, I had deliberately humiliated him. If there were people for drinks I poured for them and then said as an afterthought 'Oh Didi – help yourself' – as no doubt I did, since treating him as 'family' had become a habit in the first happy three months, and his not helping himself would have surprised me. And I took it for granted that he would clean the flat, didn't thank him when he did so, and spitefully spilt face-powder on the table he had dusted the day before.

This grievance about the cleaning was almost as alarming as the keys for what it showed of his power to repress aspects of what had happened, even in his private account. *He* had suggested that he should clean the flat. If he couldn't pay me rent, he had said, let him at least save me money by taking on this job. He had persisted until I got rid of the cleaning woman I then employed (I thought it encouraging that he wanted to earn his keep to some extent, and that it would be a good thing to foster the idea). He cleaned for one week, very well for the first two days, more and more sketchily for the remaining five, then stopped, and I had been doing it ever since. It is true that after the first day I didn't thank him, because as he had said that he wanted to do the job in order to feel less dependent, I took it that he was thinking of it *as a job* ... and now here was this incident converted into ungrateful exploitation! When the first shock of seeing his physical revulsion for me expressed in words was over, his interpretation of the lost keys and the cleaning angered me more than anything else.

I spent half an hour or more standing by his desk, leafing backwards and forwards in the diary, with the door open so that I could hear his feet on the stairs if he came in. Then I took the newspapers and went to my bedroom, leaving everything else in his room exactly as I had found it.

I was shaken enough by the contents of the diary, and even more shaken by his having left it there in that ritually tidied room baited with the Sunday papers – left it there for me to read. Not for an instant did I doubt this. Later he was to insist that it had been pure accident, and this in spite of writing, when he was describing the incident for himself, that during the weekend he had reread parts of an autobiographical book of mine and had been struck by my account of *reading my sister's diary* when I was young and finding in it something which made me 'shrivel'. He also described how when he came home that evening he had run upstairs fast 'in order to catch her in the act'. I was not to see these words until after his death, but his behaviour made their confirmation of my belief unnecessary. My only doubt concerned the degree of consciousness at work, and my fear was that he had managed to suppress it entirely. That he should be unconsciously 'possessed' by such a strong destructive impulse seemed to me truly frightening.

He returned soon after I had shut myself into my room. He came thumping up the stairs, crashed into the flat and threw open the door of his room. 'Oh god, he *has* flipped,' I thought – he was even beyond working out that he would have had a better chance to catch me at it if he had crept in quietly.

There was then silence for a few moments, followed by a creaking board in the hall and a gentle knock on my bedroom door.

'You're back?' he said, without opening the door.

'Yes.'

'Are you all right?'

'Yes, of course.'

'Oh ... good. Goodnight.'

I couldn't speak to him that night. I was trembling with anger, frozen with distaste, and more conscious than ever of the burden of responsibility. He must go, of course. That was perfectly clear. But he was sick, he was as near complete disintegration as he had ever been, and I mustn't throw him out (as I would have done if we had spoken then) with a violence which would push him further. I would wait until tomorrow, when I had calmed down, and would then write him a letter which I would give him when I came home from work.

The next morning he telephoned me at my office, while I was writing this letter.

'Are you all right?' he said again.

'Yes, I'm all right.'

'I'm glad – you see, I thought you might have read my diary.' His voice was tense, almost as though he might giggle. It made me think of a child poking at something with a stick, half fearing that it might jump at him, half challenging it to do so.

Better get it over, I thought, so I said: 'I did.'

'Oh my god!'

'It's all right, no panic. I'm writing you a letter about it and I'll leave it in the hall for you this evening. We needn't go on about it.'

'Oh my god, my god,' and he rang off.

Didi was a hoarder – so much of a hoarder that I am now convinced that he didn't destroy the manuscript of a novel at the time of the 'Henry Miller revelation', as he told me he did. He kept many drafts of everything he wrote, every letter he received, and sometimes – when he was particularly pleased with them – copies of letters he sent. He knew that as a writer he had only one subject, himself, and he saw his life as raw material for a work of literature which had only begun in his first novel. In hoarding this material he didn't cheat: he kept painful things as well as agreeable ones, and after his death I found among his papers the two letters I wrote him at this time, and one he wrote me (the last not a copy but the original; he asked for it back after our relations improved to ensure that I wouldn't show it to Luke, or so I assumed).

The letter I left in the hall for him read as follows.

You know that after you plunged off I, having simmered down, said I understood why you did it. Well, in fact I didn't understand *enough*. I'd done that thing of estimating another person's feelings from my own – attributed to you the kind of irritation and annoyance I'd been feeling about you, added an extra pinch because of your wretched position, and thought that was it.

I know now that this was underestimating. The explanation of my knowing is simple. Came back on the Sunday, wanted the Sunday papers as usual, went into your room to get them, saw open notebook on table, thought 'Good, he's been working on the children's book,' and had a peep – and then, of course, read on. For which I don't apologize since it's the kind of thing you'd do too (and most other people for that matter). And anyway, it's a good thing I did.

Because now it's quite obvious that not only were you right to feel you must go, but also you *must* go. The situation is simply intolerable for both of us. For you because you are in the nightmare situation of having to be disgusting whatever you do – if you behave and speak as you are feeling you are disgusting because of your disagreeableness, and if you don't you are even more disgusting because of your hypocrisy. And for me because it has now become impossible for me ever to behave naturally with you, now that I know fully, instead of sensing partially, what is going on in your head.

There's only one thing I want to take up – the car keys. I've never set eyes on the bloody things. Your notion that I'd recently been through the drawer you found them in is a figment of your imagination – haven't been through that drawer since clearing it for you when you came. Your supposing that I had monkeyed with the keys is a very clear symptom of how essential it is that this situation should end. It's making you *too* mad.

As soon as your £75 comes you must go, whether back to Germany or elsewhere, as you decide. If you want to go sooner I can lend you £20 on the £75 (haven't got more – sorry) but from my point of view it would be all right for you to stay a bit – it would be manageable if we left each other to our own devices and knew definitely that it was only for this short time. And when you go, you must go properly, leaving the keys and a forwarding address, but dropping any other contact – letter writing will be pointless for quite a while. What I hope – and indeed expect – is that sooner or later your mood will change and it will be possible for friendliness to go on again, but let's have no sham version of it from now on. I needn't say, need I, that I'll be glad when and if it can exist again? I know you can't help being how you are, however hard you struggle, and I'm still very fond of a good many aspects of you – it's just that it's absurd to pretend that the *present* aspect is anything but impossible to have around.

So let me know which version of going you prefer – when the cheque comes, or now, so that if the latter I can get the £20 for you. And I expect enough that this will become ancient history sooner or later, and at least some of the niceness of the past will reappear, still to want to say love from Diana.

That last sentence was a lie. I hesitated for a long time over how to end the letter, bleakly sure that whereas I might come to tolerate him again I could never in any way love him. I used those words out of what he stigmatized as my hypocrisy because I knew he was a 'case' and believed that the more destructively he behaved the more he needed to feel that love had – or could – survive.

Having read that letter he came home very drunk at one o'clock in the morning, stormed into my bedroom and started to shout at me. Didi when he lost control did literally shout, his normally attractive voice becoming a loud, hysterical barking. For the fifteen minutes or so that he was in my room it never fell to the tones of ordinary speech.

'You have done a terrible thing,' he shouted. 'A wicked and cruel thing – you've never in your life done anything so terrible as when you read my diary. It will be your fault now if I go insane, and you know it – you know how near I am to it and now you've pushed me over.' He looked like a madman – entirely distraught, decomposed, everything about him awry, his eyes glaring, his gestures frantic. His words ran together and became incoherent as he flung himself about my room.

'So why did you leave it there for me to read?' I asked. I felt cold, as though I were watching the scene from a distance. If at that moment he had pulled out a revolver and shot himself, as the cousin he liked to tell about had shot himself in front of his mother, I believe I would only have felt 'Poor little bastard, now he's done it.'

'That's idiotic, shut up with those psychological clichés,' he screamed. 'How could I put it away – Ana telephoned to say she was ready to go out to the pub, I had no time.'

That, I thought, would have been the first time he had ever put himself out half a minute for Ana, and so it would have been. He was fond of her and kind to her, but in the casual way of a brother towards a younger sister.

I expected his screaming to end with a dramatic exit not just from my room but from my flat. Instead, his last words were: 'And anyway, I can't possibly go, I haven't a penny' – and he was out of the room before I could remind him that I had offered him £20.

There had been one recurrent theme in his screaming which had increased my coldness – by which I mean not so much the coldness of hostility as an almost literally physical coldness which left me unable to do more than watch him without feeling. 'You have driven me insane and *you have hurt and humiliated yourself* unbearably.'

'I'm not *hurt*,' I interrupted at one point. 'I know you were doing something you couldn't help – '

'You must be hurt, it's impossible, you must, you *must* be hurt . . .' and I understood then that what he really meant was not that I couldn't help being hurt, but that I *had* to be, because that was what he wanted.

When I said 'I'm not hurt' I thought that I was bestirring myself out of my coldness to reassure this poor little demented creature that he had not done as much damage as he feared. Understanding his response, I recognized that not only was such reassurance pointless, but also its motive was suspect. I hadn't been thinking of this horrible moment as part of our 'game', but now I saw that both of us were still following its rules: I wasn't trying to reassure him, I was scoring. I shut up.

After a few days in which the flat was very quiet, with Didi as still as a mouse in his room until I went out, and out when I came in, I found the following letter on the hall table.

This business is having a terrible effect on me – very very much more than you can imagine, and don't say 'I know' because you don't. I shall try to explain that my diary is one thing and anyone else reading it is entirely different – there is no relationship whatever between what *I* am writing and what would be read by anyone reading it. By reading this diary you have pained and humiliated yourself – and also by reading it you have automatically made me a monster and pushed me very much towards what I have been trying to avoid – desperately, these last fifteen years or so – towards insanity as you well know – and whenever you repeat what you have read you are pushing me further towards what now seems inevitable, mental disorder.

When I started writing this particular diary was at the time when I realized I was abnormal. Not only mentally, but also in another, sexual way – and this I shall explain later. Mental disorder first. I understood my reactions to people were strange, often eerie – in fact mad. Mental disorder is often a product of, or a cause of, remarkable intelligence. I had already finished school when not yet fifteen, and was in the university, living alone. Because my family *did* realize I was insane – or nearly so – and they couldn't bear me – and as you know, didn't try (except poor Dolly). Although I suspected there was something wrong with me, I wasn't sure until I started studying at the Sorbonne. It was clear then. I couldn't live with anyone else, and my love affairs were heartbreaking catastrophes (they always have been) – catastrophes as soon as it became a matter of cohabitation. So I knew something was wrong. I tried everything to become normal. Drinking, not drinking, sport, travel, reading, being very diligent in my studies. I was good at all these things, but still I would suddenly turn against the very people who loved me, and become terribly unjust and unfair towards them. The most horrible thing was, I could *see* the injustice while doing it or saying it, and afterwards ... how terrible it was trying to explain, to say – without mentioning it – that it was a slight case of insanity.

Anyway, when I started writing I improved a lot, and then I discovered my salvation – a combination of salvation and writing. My diaries. As I mentioned already, I'd *know* that I was starting to become unjust and strange even while doing so. So, I'd sit down and write – give vent to my feelings in writing, instead of in talking or behaviour. This would simmer me down, and I'd become normal again and often shake my head at the strangeness of it all. Often, of course, I wouldn't have time to sit down and write, and there would be a surprising outburst, but it wouldn't last long. You know of course that all this causes me terrible mental depression. In depression my diary becomes hopeless because it was writing it and reading it and seeing the way I sometimes am which often used to cause depression (that is why when I was going through my last attack I wrote to you and not in the diary).

This diary, then, this medicine, this dark and innermost secret womb of mine, is something I have created to save me – and it has, but to suddenly have it exposed in this way is enough to make me go berserk. Your excuse for reading it should not have been 'Anyone would have done it' but 'I didn't know what I was doing.'

Anyway, to go on. Remember X? The way he came to you and said 'For heaven's sake, Diana, why don't you leave me alone, why do you send me voices?' Suppose that in some strange way he'd been *aware* that he was mad, and instead of coming to you he kept a diary and wrote 'That bitch Diana, sending me bloody voices all the time' – and suppose writing like that kept him from behaving abnormally towards you – he knew it was insanity, yet he wanted to express it because it is better to express it than to stifle it, so he expressed it in a diary. And then supposing you went and read his diary, what would you have thought? And how would he have thought?

Let me quote from my diary. 'She started to irritate me to shouting point. I say unconsciously, because poor Diana (or anyone else) has no inkling of what goes on in me at times, and how the most innocent remark is apt to be distorted in me, unjustly, infuriatingly – sign of my insanity.'

It is a pity you didn't read this diary properly, thoroughly and slowly. Because then it would neither have insulted nor pained you – but only made you feel sorry and you would have understood and, as I know you, would have been even more sympathetic to all my bloody messes.

Something which must have shocked you, choked you even in its brutality, must have been when I wrote ' . . . cringe at her touch'. Do you remember Gudrun and all I told you (even let you read part of that diary)? I wrote masses of things like that about her – at one time I said 'lying on the beach, she took some sand and sprinkled it on my foot, and this indirect touch, this symbolic tie, made me cringe to the very core of me'. Do you think I was writing this to be bitchy about the poor girl? Or as a demonstration of my sickness? Didn't I welcome her and cook for her and see her every day in spite of what I wrote all the time? And later we became lovers. What terrible sickness is this, then? A sickness. You read, I suppose, the last entry, where I gave this long moan about lack of sex for five months. Why? I didn't lack opportunities or a responding partner. It is this horrible thing of being unable to so much as touch a woman unless I am madly in love, or, as I have told you myself, very drunk indeed. And yet I want sex, often very much. Gudrun was around all the time, and this wanting and not wanting at the same time seems to end up by creating a monstrous fastidiousness in me – a sickness, as I have said, and anything the poor girl did I found, or forced myself to find, repulsive. The same thing has happened with you. You are not unattractive, in fact very sensually built. Because it is you I can't get disgustingly drunk and try to make love to you, the way I would to another person, and this wanting and not wanting has created this strange thing in me. But all this is my own mess. I combat it in my own way and the result is that I am normal in my behaviour and everything. Do you understand the difference now in what the contents of the diary are to me, and what they are to someone reading them?

I hope you will understand all this and feel SORRY for what you did, and never never let your friendship to me be impaired. After all, Diana, I have only you really, haven't I? I'll leave as soon as possible.

I was touched by this letter. It was full of distortions – Didi's claim, for one, that by letting off steam in his diary he was able to be 'normal in his behaviour and everything', which made me splutter aloud – and it was aimed at winning my forgiveness so that he could stay on in my flat, but it was near enough to the painful truth of his condition to make my heart ache for him.

Oddly, I almost discounted his equation of the situation between him and Gudrun with the situation between him and me. He was simply trying, I thought, to counterbalance the expressions of physical disgust in the diary, because he felt them to be the most offensive element in what I had read. I acknowledged that I too had made the comparison, and it occurred to me suddenly that violent physical distaste had woken in Didi as soon as Luke left, the moment I became technically 'available', so to speak; but still I felt that any sexuality in the tension between us was unimportant, a possibility to be considered in theory, perhaps, but not with any conviction.

It puzzles me slightly that once the first shock of seeing words on a page was over, I took so coolly Didi's 'cringing' at my mere presence, remaining fundamentally untouched by it in my sexual self-confidence. Partly this may be due to my really having uncommonly little sexual vanity. Even when I was very young it seemed to me evident that while A might be sexually attractive to B, he or she might well be unattractive to C, and long ago I learnt to accept that I was no dazzling exception to this rule; and what did this matter, considering that I was sexually attractive enough for my own purposes, in spite of it? I had had plenty of lovers in my time, and even now I knew that I pleased the only man I seriously wanted to please, so I was not vulnerable on this score; it was easy for me to relax after the first flinching, and see Didi's physical recoil from me as part of his sickness, something which left *me* untouched. As for there being distorted sexuality in that sickness (which there was, of course; Didi was being pretty accurate in that part of his letter), I was still blinded to it by the thoroughness with which I had accepted the 'old enough to be his mother' image of myself, and my lack of approach to his 'type'. I knew that I was now sexually detached from Didi, and I thought that Didi had always been sexually detached from me, so I dismissed the Gudrun–Diana equation as an attempt – a touching and generous attempt – to anoint my supposed wounds, and concentrated in dismay on Didi's evident intention of continuing to live with me.

'Didi,' I wrote,

you say 'don't say I know', but how can I not say it when you have told it so plainly? You've put it all down in that painful letter, so unless I suppose you to be lying, which you obviously aren't, I know. I know that you are a tragic person, not a beastly one – and yes, I am sorry to have precipitated this horribleness for you. I am sorry.

The condition you describe is a horror, and it isn't possible for anyone who hasn't experienced it to feel it in their bones – they can only look at it from outside. And one of the worst things in it is that it makes friendship in any ordinary, mutual, give and take sense impossible at close quarters (as you have often said before now, with your talk of 'no one can stick me for more than three weeks'). I would like to say 'Because you have told me, and because I have understood what you have said, and because I am sorry with all my heart, stay here.' But I can't because I'm not up to it.

It is not possible for two people to live under the same roof for a long time unless each of them is able to allow the other space, so to speak – give the other a certain amount of attention and consideration. And at anything but surface level you, except during your better times (like in the first three months you were here) can't do it because you are so deeply bogged down in your own state. The worst shock you gave me – worse even than the diary – was driving home that evening after we'd been with X when you said savagely 'You're in the position of power' at a time when I was so far from thinking about you and me, so deep in something completely removed from that and very painful and important to me, that it seemed absolutely *incredible* that anyone should have so little of the ordinary sensitivity of friendship that he couldn't be aware of it and allow for it. It was that night that I realized you couldn't be a friend except from time to time, only someone I wanted to help because I was fond of him and he was in a mess, which is different.

I've got a bad vanity, which is the vanity of wanting to feel that I am a nice person rather than a nasty one. Therefore I wanted to go on being the same towards you in spite of that disappointment, and I've tried hard to do so. But it's bloody difficult – too difficult, it turns out, for me – to do that when you can't help seeing that the person opposite you is seeing you all the time as stupid, wildly irritating, displeasing. Do you know that it's months since you have been able to look at me except in fleeting, hostile glances, while you talk to me? I expect you do. And months since you've been able to prevent yourself from snapping a contradiction to every lightest thing I say? Yes, of course you know it, because you know your own symptoms so well, but you may not know quite to what an extent I was aware of it, and how extraordinarily lowering it is as an experience *whatever the reason for it.* I could say to myself till I was blue in the face 'This is only Didi being as he can't help being, it's what he means when he says people can't stick him for long, it's the dreadful thing which happens to him, not something he can help' – and I realized enough of it to say that to myself many times, long before reading this letter which has made it even more clear. But however much I said it, it didn't prevent it from being depressing and unpleasant to go through, so however hard I tried your presence here stopped being a very real pleasure to me and gradually became something to endure.

Probably the person who could live with you through the bad times as well as the good would have to be totally unselfish – make no claims for his or her self at all – which

God knows is far from true about me. I should loathe to lose my affection for you, but I could if this went on, however wicked and unjust of me this would be. That's why I felt that reading the diary was a good thing, because it tipped me into saying you must leave. The whole thing was becoming false on my side and obviously more painful on your side, so to have something happen which made it violently obvious that this was happening, would at least end it.

I don't in the least want my friendship for you to be impaired. I want to withdraw on to neutral territory, so to speak, have a rest, and let everything I value in you come up again in my mind, and my concern and affection for you come alive again. I'm a poor thing to be the only thing you have, as events have proved, but I don't want to stop being at least something you have, for the reason that you have been a lot for me, too, and I liked having you in my life so want to go on having you there. If the strain is taken off I'm perfectly sure this will happen. It's really a matter of hoping for practical ways of taking the strain off, such as the BBC providing you with a job – because if you don't go I shall fail you hopelessly, Didi. It's appalling to know it and to say it, but I can't not, because it's true – as you must realize from the extent to which I have failed you already. I've already reached the stage of being well and truly unable to meet the claims which you, because of what you describe in your letter, inevitably make on people at close quarters, and I can't patch or cobble up my resources for more than a very little longer.

So that's how it is. You are burdened with something terrible, and I'm not up to it in the circumstances. 'Sorry' is an inadequate word for what I feel when you show me your abyss – it's more like misery and self-loathing because I'm not able to work a miracle on myself and become someone who can be unaffected by everything you do or say, and who doesn't want to live her own dim existence in her own dim way, alone. It's a nightmare that anyone should suffer as much as you do without someone else being able to take off at least part of it, and I'm ashamed of not being able to.

That, I thought, *must* end it. It was as exact a description as I could manage of the toll the situation was taking on me, and surely it made clear that I had gone beyond appeals to sympathy, that I had reached the point of rejection. The level of sincerity on which it was written was split. I wholly meant it when I said that he must go, while I only knew that I ought to mean it when I blamed myself for my failure to endure him any longer (and in addition exaggerated that aspect of my feelings in an attempt to avoid 'punishment' and 'blame', and to make the rejection as little painful as possible); but it seemed to me that the parts of the letter which were not wholly sincere were nevertheless true, and that they therefore needed to be written. Surely Didi must be able to see, when he read it, that it wasn't him that I had come to hate, but the situation; and that I *had* come to hate the situation so that there was no alternative to ending it. And immediately after writing the letter I thought of 'a practical way of taking the strain off'. If Didi could find a room to rent for £3 or £4, I could let my spare room again for £5 a week, as I used to do, pay his rent for him – and still be better off. I suggested this in a separate note and felt that the end was in sight.

I left both letter and note in the hall, and they disappeared, so Didi must have taken them. I waited for him to react. Nothing happened. A day went by – another day – another and another. He was always out when I came home from work, returning very quietly long after I had gone to bed, and he was always asleep when I left in the mornings. He was going to ignore the letter. He wrote for himself at this time 'I am behaving like what I am – a creep. Creep into the flat, creep out of it ...'; and I listened to the faint sounds of the creeping and thought with resignation 'I must be mad.' If I were to get rid of him, what I must do now was to go into his room at whatever time suited me, whether he was asleep or not, and say: 'Didi, you have read my letter and it is intolerable that you have not yet acted on it. Out!' – and that I was incapable of doing. Simply incapable – I didn't know (still don't know) why.

The situation began to seem to me – and this is often my undoing at times when I ought to act – comic. What a pity, I thought, that I didn't have a big house instead of a small flat: a shabby big house built of wood, with lilac bushes and raspberry canes struggling through the nettles in the garden – a Russian country house. The house in my mind came out of a story by Turgenev – I can't remember which one – and was the sort of house in which the cast of characters might include an old man in carpet slippers who appears to be unrelated to the family: an old man slightly on the margin of the action whose presence is unquestioned even though people are often annoyed with him. He lives there until he dies, and perhaps his death sparks a moment of truth among the other characters: they pause uneasily for a moment, facing guilt. Didi, I thought, half despairing, half laughing, was going to be my old man in carpet slippers. He always said that when he read about Russians he felt that he was reading about Egyptians, and I reckoned that he might just as well feel that he was reading about me, too.

Something, however, had happened as a result of the explosion over the diary. The comedy was accentuated by the fact that it had brought about some kind of release in Didi, the first sign of which was the end of his five months' abstinence from love. At a time when it seemed to me and my allies (my cousin and Sheila, who spent much time and energy debating with me what was to be done about him) that his relations with me must be his dominant preoccupation, he chose to fall in love in a particularly 'Didi-ish' way.

The girl was very young and only moderately pretty, but she was unusually composed for her age, and although she didn't wear black she spoke good French. This was only natural since she was half French and had been brought up in France, but to Didi it made her overpoweringly 'elegant' and superior to the clod-hopping women of England. To us, the onlookers, it seemed that in falling madly in love with this girl at first sight Didi was ducking his dilemma with me with an almost sublime insouciance, but his own description of the beginning of the affair reveals that this was not wholly true.

I didn't – couldn't – see Diana or anyone else in the house. Crept in and out, shrinking as soon as I passed the front door, busied myself translating, drinking, making sure my *physical* presence was at least reduced to the minimum. Terrible for both of us. She is, however, endowed with an unbelievable greatness – she is beginning to forgive me. And my gratitude would have made me run amok if something else hadn't suddenly happened. Ah Didi ... Didi ... Love ... love is here again. I love and am loved. It is glorious. I am basking in it. I even sigh with my own secret happiness, and inexplicably I have become careless about all my material worries. I don't care any more. Even if I get thrown out of England – so what? I am too happy to care. [There follows a description of his meeting with the girl, and an account of the rest of that evening] ... I was in my most charming, debonair, attractive mood, the one only real despair can induce (despair because of the incident with Diana, weighing very heavily on me). From despair in a gay mood to recklessness and madness. Went into an off-licence. No one. I tap. No one heard, or if they heard they didn't bother. A man quarrelling with someone inside. Facing me were three gallon jars of wine. I took a gallon flask of Burgundy, worth about £3. I'll never make a good thief because going out, drunk as I was, my heart was knocking so hard, my teeth chattering. Into the car and away fast. Just as we passed the shop two men emerged looking round madly – for a pedestrian. Usually I have a terrible conscience when I do something like that, but I didn't this time. But I was still shaking a bit and bumped slightly into another car – but moved away quickly. Absolute recklessness ... [and later, when they were dancing in a restaurant] suddenly she was in my arms and we were kissing and hugging madly – madly. We spent about two hours there, kissing and hugging. We spoke in French and how I wanted to scream (because I haven't for so long) '*Je t'aime, je t'aime*' – et d'ailleurs je l'aimais. Enfin. Drove home singing.

Didi made no attempt to conceal this love, which lasted for about three weeks. He brought the girl home to show her off to my cousin, they met in espresso bars and held hands, he gave her a rose, they walked on Hampstead Heath. It was like a very old-fashioned affair between teenagers, until one evening when he kept her in his room all night – the first time he had spent a night in the flat with a woman while I was there. That was the end.

She spent the night with me, in my arms, and apart from anything else I looked ten years younger next morning. But this is going too fast, because we did have words in my bed, and it wasn't very satisfactory. In the morning she was rather cold and I had to change the wheel of her car and it wasn't very friendly really. Anyway, I didn't make a date with her. 'Well,' I thought, 'that's it. Let *me* end it, not she.' *Pauvre* Didi. I think of the end before it even starts – and this, in a way, makes the end happen.

From this girl he went on to others, although without imagining love: the mood of 'fastidiousness' was over and he was fucking anyone he could lay hands on with manic energy and almost no pleasure ('My eyes on the alarm clock over her shoulder to see how long I lasted'), and drinking more and more heavily. He was out every evening, came home at three or four in the morning, began to look like Lazarus, and the line of empty whisky bottles on his bookshelf grew by one every day. He had managed to struggle through a piece of translation from the German, a boring and badly written article of which he made a good job (he could always make a good job of anything written if only he could bring himself to do it), and had been paid £40, all of which went on whisky. He was supporting a feverish euphoria entirely on alcohol, and with every day the means came nearer to defeating the end as his hangovers plunged him deeper and deeper. I didn't then *know* that every sober moment brought him thoughts of suicide, but I suspected it, and after a week or so of this I knew that I must at least try to force him into a situation where he might sober up. If he were out of the house and on his own again it might do it – and anyway I would be rid of my old man in carpet slippers, I can't deny the presence of that thought. So one evening when, un-usually, he was in his room when I came home from work, I found myself able to do what until then I had been unable to do.

I knew that unless I spoke at once my courage would fail, so I spoke as soon as I was in his room, without preliminaries, although I made my voice as gentle as I could.

'Didi,' I said, 'you know when I said in that letter that I wanted you to leave and that I would pay the rent of a room for you? Well, I really did mean that.'

We were at opposite sides of the room, he sitting on his bed. He stood up and turned his head sideways, his chin up, his eyes hooded – a forced moment of intense and haughty composure – and then, without warning, he stumbled across the room, threw his arms round me, and was sobbing with his head on my shoulder.

'I don't want to die,' he sobbed. 'I don't want to die – life can be so beautiful, oh god why do I do this, why do I always have to *destruct* everything I love, why must I die?' The 'child of eight' was crying hopelessly in my arms. The truth of the situation had emerged.

There was nothing for it but to accept it, and to comfort him. The lack of alternative was so obvious that I experienced something like relief. It was easy to stroke him and to murmur 'Hush darling, hush – never mind, love, it'll be all right, you're not going to die' – easy because natural, the only answer. I steered him to a chair, sat him down, fetched him a handkerchief, kissed him (careful to do so very lightly, and only on his forehead, because in spite of the abandon of his tears I had felt something come alert in him at the touch of my hands, whether the old repugnance or something new I wasn't sure, and I didn't want to find out). I went to make a pot of tea, and he sat waiting for it in trusting docility, all defences down.

Now, I thought, the moment had come when I could do something with him. Now I could get him to agree to see a doctor. I had made enquiries about the treatment of depression and I knew that the chances of its being successful were only slight, but if a chance existed it should be taken, and at least he might become interested in the treatment and pass the time during which he was receiving it more profitably than he was doing at present.

'Darling,' I said, 'it's silly to pretend that you aren't iller than ever, isn't it?'

'I know, I know.'

'You don't have any faith in psychiatrists, I know, but I've heard of an unorthodox kind which sounds much more sensible than any other – ' and I told him what I knew about the work of Drs Laing and Cooper. Whether either of them would take on a depressive I was unsure, but they would at least be kind. A friend of Didi's who was training to be a psychiatrist had recently become so worried for him that she had telephoned me and told me that I ought to get him hospitalized, and although I knew that her concern was justified I had jibbed at the idea of forcing him (how, anyway?) into a psychiatric ward where, I was convinced, his resentful misery would be far too intense for him to benefit from any treatment he received. He wouldn't stay in such a place for a day unless he were forcibly restrained, and that I would subject no one to. No doctor could help him unless he met him as an intelligent being, by his own consent. Until this moment he had refused to let me speak more than two words on the subject without going out of the room, but now at last he might be ready to listen to news of doctors who would think of him as *him*, and not as a mad person.

He consented to listen, even asking questions, although he kept returning to 'But I *know* they can't do any good.' Then I said: 'Listen, I want to make a bargain with you. If you will agree to *try* seeing a doctor, at least, then you can stay here. It's simply not fair on me to refuse – you know how awful it's been – so will you promise, and I'll make an appointment for you?'

Didi then did something of which he was too ashamed to write in his diary, although his description of this occasion was otherwise full and accurate. He told me that why he was so sure that a psychiatrist couldn't help him was because he had a tumour on the brain. I asked him how he knew, and he said that X-rays had shown it.

I knew that sometimes – twice so far, since he had been staying with me – he had appalling headaches which continued for two or three days, increasing all the time, and that he dealt with them by going to the out-patients' department of a hospital and having, he said, a lumbar puncture. I had naturally thought with horror of a brain tumour the first time this happened, and had urged him to have an X-ray taken. He had pooh-poohed my anxiety and had explained the trouble by saying that after one of his car smashes a small fragment of skull-bone stuck out, like a splinter from a plank, and that from time to time pressure had to be relieved as a result. He swore that he had taken medical advice on it both in Germany and in London, and that he had been told that unless it got much worse it was wiser to put up with it than to have an operation. Now he said that he had told me this to spare me, and that in fact a tumour had been diagnosed.

What the truth was I do not know (nothing was reported after his autopsy), but there were certainly times when he *feared* that he had a tumour. Once, in his diary, when for some reason he decided that his headaches were the result of sexual frustration, he expressed great relief at this conclusion; and on another occasion he wrote: 'At times I literally want to open my head, put my hands inside and squeeze and push and make a paste of the whole lot. Hope this is not going to be the reality – not my hands, someone else's. I am, alas, often very sure that there is something very wrong and fatal in my brain.' What was certainly untrue was the story he now produced of the X-ray which had shown a tumour. This was no more than an inspired embroidery on his fears to make sure that my sympathy was captured for good.

It neither worked nor failed to work. I went through the motions of concern, pointing out that if he had a tumour it was even more necessary to see a doctor, but I was inclined not to believe him. I must *allow* for this being the truth, I thought, but it was probably a safe bet not to become anguished over it because it was – if only marginally – more likely to be an invention than the reality, and an unnecessary invention at that. Given the mental mess he was in, no physical trouble was needed to keep me hooked.

One of the few things I laughed at when I came to read the whole of Didi's diary was the last word on this incident, which belongs to him: 'I didn't cry solely because of my miserable insanity and plight, but I cried for Diana too. I could see that she would never shake this awful burden of myself away from her.'

'Crisis Diana' ended for good about a week later. There had been affection between Didi and me in the intervening days. I had written to Dr Cooper and had received a kind answer (although this was to come to nothing, because after half promising that he would visit the doctor, Didi slithered out of it), and Didi had again collapsed into tears and been comforted. He was drinking no less frantically, but he had suddenly become willing to bring his hangovers home to me openly instead of hiding them in his room.

I was more worried over him than I had ever been, but at the same time I felt 'better in myself'. Instead of making him 'cringe', my physical presence had suddenly become benign to him, so that he sought it as a hurt child runs for comfort to its nurse or mother, and it was a relief to be rid of the disgusting image of myself which he had been reflecting, even though I hadn't believed in it. It was also a relief of a different kind – an unstoppering, as opposed to the removal of pressure from outside – to be able to indulge myself again in expressions of affection and gestures of comfort, even though I was unable to see how they could do any good.

This feeling of relief from pressure may have been the reason why I enjoyed far more than I expected a literary cocktail party to which I had to go. I went straight from my office, and expected to be back in the flat by about 8.30. I had not mentioned the party to Didi.

Instead of leaving early I stayed till the end, and went on after the party to have supper with friends. We sat talking until after midnight, and we drank a great deal. I didn't realize how drunk I was until I was in the taxi on the way home and noticed that things were rocking slightly. 'Heavens!' I thought, 'it's at least twenty years since things last rocked – I must be hugely drunk,' and this was confirmed when I reached the flat by a mad burst of domestic energy. On the few occasions when I am so drunk that there is a chance I'll end by passing out, I usually go through a stage of euphoric energy during which I suddenly and perfectly efficiently do something like washing my hair or preparing a stew, knowing as I do it that I must be brisk and get it finished before the next stage sets in.

This time the energy went into doing the laundry – next day was clean-sheet day. Didi was out, so after I had stripped and made my bed I did his, wrote out the laundry list and packed up the box, pleased with myself at making such practical use of this stage of the drunkenness. Then I decided that there was enough of the energy left to see me through my bath, and I got myself undressed and bathed with undiminished competence. Coming out of the bathroom I bumped the wall and thought 'Oho, here we go! We're nearly into stage two,' and it occurred to me that although I was still feeling well and cheerful, I might be drunk enough to vomit later on.

I remembered – although I hadn't thought of it for several years – that a previous lodger had once had a sick child to stay and had bought a chamber-pot for this emergency, which he had left behind and which had been at the back of my storage cupboard ever since. Infinitely clever, I felt, at remembering this pot, and cleverer still as I went down on hands and knees and burrowed my way into the cupboard to find it. I would put it beside my bed. Then, supposing I had to be sick and proved to be too far gone to get to the lavatory, it wouldn't matter. I knew that I was grinning and wagging my head in fatuous pride at having thought up this precaution, and the more I knew it the more I grinned. It was an amusing and agreeable drunkenness.

Indeed it was so agreeable that I was spared not only nausea, but even what had seemed the inevitable vertigo on lying down. I was ready to sit up again and to stare hard at my chest of drawers in order to keep the bed still, but instead I was out as soon as my head touched the pillow.

The next thing I knew was that my bedroom door had opened and that the light had been switched on. 'People are coming into my room,' I thought distinctly, without moving or opening my eyes because I couldn't. Then the light went off and the door clicked shut, and with relief I thought 'People gone away again – good.' I didn't even speculate as to who 'people' were or what they were doing. I was sunk so deep in a deliciously warm and dark well of sleep that anything beyond the registering of a sound or movement was impossible.

Perhaps – very likely – it was only a few seconds later that the side of my mattress was depressed, but I had been down to the bottom of the lovely well again, so it might have been hours for all I knew. 'People' hadn't gone away again, it seemed: they were in my room and had just sat down on my bed at a level with my waist. After what may have been quite a long time it occurred to me that I ought to open my eyes and try to see who 'they' were. I sleep with my curtains open and it was not a dark night, so I recognized the silhouette of the silent figure at once, and with a renewal of relief. It was Didi – I needn't do anything about *him*. He appeared to be naked, which was odd, but I couldn't be bothered with details and I shut my eyes again.

Then, tiresomely, he spoke.

'What's that horrible thing doing there?' he said.

I had no idea what he was talking about. What horrible thing? He was drunk, of course, and I needn't answer.

'What's that horrible thing doing there?' he said again. 'What's it doing?' And no sooner had I sunk back into oblivion than his voice dragged me up again – 'that horrible thing'? What a bore he was being.

At last I heaved my eyelids up again, and this time he made a movement with his foot as he asked his parrotlike question, kicking the chamber-pot. Understanding enlivened me a little, and for the first time I spoke.

'I'm drunk,' I said. 'Thought I might be sick.'

There was the sound of a match: Didi had lit a cigarette. He was going to stay there. It didn't seem that he wanted to cry, but perhaps he was going to talk. He'd been talking a lot lately.

'What do you want to talk about?' I asked. I still hadn't moved a muscle and I had opened my eyes only twice. If he wanted to talk, let him; I could sink back into the well while he was doing so. He said: 'Sh, don't talk.'

He must have smoked all his cigarette because there was only a tiny butt in the chamber-pot next morning. Then I felt my mattress rise as he stood up, and I heard him say: 'I'm glad you're drunk. Let me get in.'

I found that I could move after all. It was possible to edge myself over a few inches to make room for him, and the effort enlivened me again so that when he was lying beside me I repeated 'What do you want to talk about?' Again he said 'Sh, don't talk.' And a few moments later he turned towards me, put an arm over me, and began to stroke my naked back very slowly, from the nape of my neck down to my buttocks. God bless my soul, I thought dreamily, he's going to make love to me!

The sensation of his stroking was delicious, perfectly in tune with the relaxation of my body. I was too nearly out to experience any specifically sexual reaction, but warmth and softness, softness and warmth – let them go on, part of the softness and warmth I was in already. The utter physical relaxation which is supposed to enable a drunk person to fall down a flight of stairs without hurting himself: that was what I was in, and it was blissful. When Didi moved to lie on top of me and pushed my legs apart with his, it came to me dimly that I was so far from being sexually excited that he might not be able to get further, but I didn't see what I could do about that, and anyway he managed it after a while, and there we were, Didi and I, making love.

It was entirely agreeable, gentle and tender. As it went on more of my consciousness surfaced, but not much of it, only enough for me to move my hands so that I was holding his shoulders and caressing his head and neck, and to know that I was glad that he didn't want to kiss me on the mouth – we must both be smelling disgustingly of stale drink and smoke. He gave me light kisses round the face and on the neck and breasts, murmuring 'You're so beautiful, so beautiful' – ritual words, nothing to do with me, I understood and accepted them as such. And I understood, too, that I mustn't murmur in return the words which would have come out if I had opened my mouth, which would have been: 'My little one, my baby.' It was, however, pleasant to say them to myself, to let tenderness move my hands, and to feel with sleepy amusement that what I had once wanted was now happening, and that although I no longer wanted it, it was in some mysterious way not without meaning:

that this once, at least, Didi and I were expressing in a loving way – were perhaps dreaming? – the secret which lay between us.

My drunkenness had been restricting the range of my consciousness, but it hadn't been distorting it. Now, as activity gradually widened the range of what I could perceive, it was my ordinary self perceiving it and I knew that it would be a pity to spoil what was happening by letting it go on too long. Tenderness would soon be counteracted by the weariness of my un-aroused body, so I had better end this love-making by faking a climax and bringing Didi to his. When that was done there was a moment of quite sober anxiety in which I feared that he might pass out and remain in my bed all night, but when I whispered 'Bed too small' he sat up and started to scrabble at something near his feet. 'What you doing?' I mumbled. 'Trying to put on these bloody underpants,' he said. 'Why?' -- 'Must observe the decencies.' Yes – he certainly was very drunk indeed, perhaps even drunker than I was. I was asleep again within a few seconds of his leaving my room.

I woke next morning without a hangover, which was mysterious, but full of anxiety. It was impossible to regret anything so pleasant and tender, but what would be the consequences? For me it would remain an isolated incident, something to remember as slightly mad, more than slightly comic and wholly delightful; but what would it be for Didi? Would he recoil from it in sick horror? Would he (oh lord!) choose to launch into fantasy passion from it? I'd better do what I could to control the situation without delay.

It was a Saturday morning – the morning when Didi always, even during our worst hostilities, offered to take me shopping in his car. As soon as he heard me moving about he called from his room 'Do you want to go shopping?' I opened his door to say yes. He was lying in bed, looking a little sheepish but relaxed, and said: 'I drank a whole bottle of rum last night after leaving the pub.'

'You must have been even drunker than me,' I said. 'You'd better lay off rum in the future.'

'That's not a very nice thing to say.'

'I suppose not – but you know quite well how I mean it, don't you?'

'Yes, perhaps – ' and we went shopping together in a normal and friendly way. Didi made only two other references to our love-making that day. During lunch he said kindly 'You've got an astonishingly young body for your age, you know,' to which I answered 'Thank you, love, it's not too bad'; and after the meal, while I was washing up, he came quickly into the kitchen, looking tense, and said: 'Promise me one thing. Promise that this is one thing you'll never tell Luke about.'

'Of course I won't, I promise.' (I was already mulling in my head the written account, as exact as possible, which I was going to show Luke one day.)

'The trouble is, I *know* you ... Look, tell him about a lover, if you want to, but don't say it was me.'

'I *promise* I won't tell him.'

Didi gave me a sceptical look, smiled crookedly, and went back to his room.

After that I knew that he was going to make no more of the incident than I would, and the few references he made to it during the next few days were light and natural. He offered to put a bolt on my door in case, on another drunken night, he might come in again. He even bought a bolt, but we found that the moulding round the door prevented us from fixing it, and when I said 'Never mind, you'll never again catch me equally drunk, and if I just asked you to go away you would, wouldn't you?' he said 'Yes, of course' (which he did, the only other time he came in, about four days later). And on another occasion he said: 'It's a funny thing, you know, but since that night all the tension's gone' – and it had.

Less than a week afterwards I was having a drink with him in his room while he was preparing to go out, because such friendliness was now possible again. When he opened his cupboard I saw a jacket I had never seen before.

'What's that jacket?'

'My mother sent it to me, X brought it when he came over.'

'Why do you never wear it?'

'It doesn't fit — or at least, I don't think it does.'

'Put it on and let me see.'

He took the jacket out and put it on, examining the fit in the mirror.

'Actually,' he said, 'it's a very *nice* jacket. I don't know why I thought it was no good. It's only that the sleeves need shortening, isn't it? And the material is very good.'

He stood there smoothing the material with his hand, looking at himself with pleasure, then turned and gave me a little display of how elegant he was, enjoying the jacket his mother had sent; and I thought suddenly: 'Now that he's at last been to bed with his mother, he can wear her jacket.'

And if this were a work of fiction that would be the end of the story.

6 'It had to happen ...'

It was, of course, only the end of one chapter in the story: the chapter about Didi and myself. I may be right – I believe I am – in thinking that our relationship touched nerves close to the centre of his wound, but it would have been naive to suppose (and by then I knew Didi too well to suppose it) that resolving the tensions in that particular relationship could alter the pattern of his life as a whole.

For the next year or so, however, Didi appeared to be better. Luke returned from abroad a few weeks after 'Crisis Diana' ended, I was happy, Didi plunged into a whirl of activity, and my flat seemed to have reverted to the cheerfulness of his first months in England. He started to accumulate new friends so fast that he had trouble keeping up with old ones, and running two or three girls simultaneously. He was still able to say primly, as a reproof to me, 'I don't understand people who are cynical and matter-of-fact about sex. It's impossible for me to make love unless I'm madly in love – which is why I have to be madly in love so often,' but during this period the alternative of being drunk served him well and often. It was a year before he was 'madly in love' again, and even then he managed, with a desperate struggle and help from a stroke of luck, not to topple over into the anguish which usually followed his full-blown passions.

But his more casual affairs were less of a contradiction to his belief about himself than they appeared: he saw them as a clever 'managing' of the perils of his temperament. Every new girl he took to bed provided him with something he was starving for – reassurance as to his own attractiveness – and each time he 'went off' a girl before she 'went off' him, he saw it not as a failure of passion or as being unkind to that girl, but as a skilful avoidance of suffering. He had managed, this time, not to be 'madly in love' – he had beaten it for once! And meanwhile he was able to avoid seeing himself as unfeeling because what we called 'the Victorian maiden' in him ('It's very complicated', he said one day, 'to be a lecherous old Wog on the outside and a Victorian maiden inside') – the 'Victorian maiden' was kept happy by the only unsexual passion I ever saw him go through.

As soon as our crisis was over he began to adore a married friend of ours who had been extraordinarily kind to him. He was shy of her, even in awe of her, and never expected her to respond. He wanted only to see her and to please her, and that she should let him know that she knew he was in love with her, which she obligingly did. It was in a way the most unreal of all his loves, yet when I had read his full account of it I saw that in another way it was the most real. This woman was the only one he saw as existing in her own right, the only one on whose behalf he felt genuine concern. If she was sad, he truly wanted to cheer her up; if she was ill he went to considerable trouble to help her in practical ways. His usual method for conjuring up sympathy for other people's suffering was to picture it as being like his own: 'Poor so and so, he's in a dep, how I feel for him' – 'Poor such and such, my heart bleeds for her, I know so well what it's like not to be loved in return' (the sufferers would sometimes have been surprised to learn what troubles were being attributed to them). But Didi recognized that his 'pure love' was a person very different from himself, and made genuine efforts to understand her. This wholly romantic and yet genuine love was too frail to last for long, but while it endured it did more than prevent him from becoming self-disgusted when he considered his other affairs; it took him a little way out of himself and gave him many moments of happiness; and it was one of the very few loves in his life which tapered off with little more than reasonable regret, not anguish.

This woman helped Didi to the one practical achievement of his last years. She was able to give him the necessary introductions and wise advice on how to use them when he decided to visit Israel after the Six Day War.

When the war broke out, Didi's surface reaction was to break into strident Egyptian chauvinism, screaming that Israel was the aggressor and that Nasser was right, it was the Americans and the British who were beating the Arabs, the combined forces of Western capitalism of which Israel was the willing pawn. He wrote otherwise in his diary.

For ten long years Nasser has exhorted us to spend our money, our harvests, our goods on the Army. He has persuaded the Egyptian people that it was imperative for them to possess an Army. And we – or rather *they* – bled and bled to achieve this. Now he has challenged Israel to show her might. And she did. She overran us, Jordan and all the combined Arab armies (except Algerian) in *twenty-four* hours! Yes, just walked all over us. To cover this utter and complete humiliation Nasser invented the excuse that America and Britain supported Israel's military force. I am no lover of those two countries' policies, but even I felt disgusted, more humiliated and insulted, by this cheap lie. And so, after thirteen years or more, he has turned out to be unreliable, incompetent, dishonest. It is all disgusting, sad and full of shame ... I loathe him absolutely.

For a few weeks before, during and after the Six Day War Didi was living not in my flat but in a room for which I paid the rent, as I had suggested earlier. It came about easily enough now that the tension between us was over, as a result of a short and unimportant squabble which left no ill feelings, and he was prevented from being forlorn by his attachment to his 'pure love'. I therefore saw little of him while he was deciding to try to get to Israel, and his diary records only that he had made the decision and had, astonishingly, been granted a visa. There is a hailstorm of exclamation marks after the statement, the explanation that 'it will be an Egyptian interviewing the Israelis gimmick', and the comment: 'Since I have given up smoking I have become very much more active and alive, and I really don't want to have to kill myself NOW ...'

This passage is embedded in page after page of writing on what really mattered to him: his casual adventures, and his love. And these pages suggest the truth of the matter. He was not so gay as he seemed to be. 'The *cafard*' was beginning to sneak up on him again and was driving him to seek refuge as usual in drunkenness, and he was terrified that this serene and idyllic love might at any moment turn and sink the usual poisonous fangs of misery into his heart. He had not the strength of will to break out of the situation without some extraordinary stimulus, and the drama of the plunging off to Israel at a time when no one believed it possible for an Egyptian to do so was heaven-sent.

Once he had his visa, he would approach a newspaper and propose that it should commission him to write articles on what was happening in Israel after the war, from the Arab point of view. I was sceptical about his bringing it off, although I didn't say so, and was therefore all the more delighted when he did. Both *The Times* and the *Observer* were prepared to put up money for his journey against articles which he would write when there, or after he came back.

There were some dicy moments when he almost abandoned the idea because the money he was offered was less than his wildly exaggerated idea of what it might be, but his 'pure love' and I combined to persuade him that he was not being cheated, and he came back to my flat, quivering with exhilaration and nervousness and full of affection, for a family send-off. After we had eaten 'a feast' and helped him pack he relaxed a little. We had been lavish with encouragement and congratulation, and because he knew that we knew he felt the adventure to be something of a con, a larky atmosphere was distilled in which it could be admitted that it was *funny* that he was going to be 'our correspondent' for *The Times*. To me and his love he could admit that he had no idea of how to set about it, and he could even (for once!) ask for advice.

By the end of the evening euphoria prevailed. This, he was sure, was the beginning of great things. It was true that the money now in his wallet would be consumed by the expenses of the trip, so that he would come home empty-handed, but if he sent back good stories other work would be sure to follow: he would become established as an expert on the Middle East.

People have become established as experts after setting out with considerably less knowledge of their subject than Didi had, and without being able to write so well. Other articles, other work, *could* follow, and given the stimulus of success it was surely *possible* that he might become truly involved and be drawn almost in spite of himself out of his claustrophobic nightmare? Only the wings of illusion could carry him into such a project, but if they beat strongly enough they might – they just might – take him to a point where they ceased to be necessary.

Late that night Didi turned to me and said: 'Now I shall have some money at last, so I can come back to be your lodger, can't I? I mean your proper, paying lodger – you wouldn't mind me here if I was that?'

I hesitated, and that was when the trite image of the wings of illusion came to me. I must not cause them to falter. 'Yes,' I said. 'Of course you must come back here. You know quite well that of all the proper lodgers I could possibly have, you are the one I'd like best.'

And oh dear oh dear, I thought as I went to bed, trying in shame to smother the thought but not succeeding: oh dear oh dear, this will turn out to be where we came in.

Given Didi's condition, he performed an heroic feat in Israel. He moved around, he interviewed people, he disciplined himself against prejudice, and he wrote the articles he had undertaken to write. They were not exceptionally good but they were presentable, and that was more of an achievement in Didi than a flash of brilliance would have been. There was never any question about his being able to write, and to write well, if he were moved by his own drives. The question lay in whether he could turn out a piece of writing *as a job* – a competent piece of writing taking into account requirements other than those dictated by his own emotions − and this he did. To anyone who didn't know him well it must have seemed natural that an intelligent and gifted writer with a built-in concern for the Middle East should be able to write pieces like these, but to those who knew him best they, and the few other pieces he wrote and talks he gave after his return, were a joyful surprise, proof that if only − if only − certain elements in him could be overcome he could be grown-up, he could manage, he could live.

To begin with Israel itself did much to overcome the destructive elements. It was a long time since Didi had looked outwards, and Jerusalem made him do so.

I'd happened to jump on a bus which took me straight to the most fascinating place I have seen for years and years − to one of the gates of the Old City. A terminal for a thousand buses, Arab and Jewish, an agglomeration of faces, types, religions, languages, needs, trades, voices.

There I stood, then. An avalanche of titillations enlivened me. Every face I saw I recognized, knew and had something in common with. The seller of [illegible], carrying his elaborate piece of glass and polished brass on a strap over his shoulders − the pathetic man standing behind five bottles of Coca Cola (the economics of such earnings are beyond me − absolutely) or the vendor of three maize cobs, boiling them away in a tin. The religious representatives, agents as it were of some central god, competing madly like so many branches of the same firm undercutting each other in the same square − rabbis, ugly and dirty − some youthful, beardless pre-rabbis (I suppose, I am so ignorant of all that) with a strand of hair curling down above each ear of which they perpetually try to make a ringlet − Greek Orthodox priests, Coptic Orthodox − which you recognise at once because you feel they haven't washed for a year. A muslim muezzin, a Sunni − slightly cleaner, or anyway more elegant in his abayieh. Swedes, French, English, Irish, not belonging but watching on the outskirts. And I was suddenly in the midst of all this ...

For the first two of the three weeks he spent in Israel his diary remained full of portraits, reported conversations, descriptions of incidents, speculations on the significance of what he saw. It was lively, intelligent and objective. He was not, however, freed from the necessity to drink, and he found himself unable to sleep unless he took pills; and during the third week the spell stopped working. 'The *cafard*' began to re-appear: he started to find an old friend he'd come across with joy unbearably irritating; fits of heartache over his 'pure love' attacked him, so that 'Why no letter from her?' became more important than 'Am I going to get an interview with Dayan?'; he began to leave undone things which he knew he ought to do, to get more drunk more often, to sniff around for gambling companions. At the end of the three weeks he left the country with a hangover, having lost £35 at poker the night before, and feeling – so he recorded in his diary – 'really glad to be leaving'.

He came back to my flat and neither of us bothered to refer to – or even, on my side, to think much about – his being there as a 'proper lodger'. He worked on the articles resulting from his journey, and to his already numerous friends was added a group of left-wing Israeli expatriates who injected shots of unrealistic political activity into his social life so that he could often say that he was going to a meeting, not to a party. I felt that it must do him good to believe that some of his activities had a purpose beyond that of merely passing the time, but I know now that he didn't really believe it. I hardly bothered to answer the telephone because calls were always for Didi, and so was the ringing of the front-door bell. The bathroom smelt fragrant almost every evening, his step was almost always brisk (with a little skip as he went through the front gate of the garden), and if he wasn't with his pub cronies, his Israeli friends, an amusing-disgusting group of rich Egyptians who had turned up, an equally amusing-disgusting bunch of rich young English people, his other pub cronies, the old friends in Hampstead, the new friends in Richmond, the old friends in north Kensington, the new friends in Putney – if he wasn't with one lot or another of this astonishing variety of friends, all of whom enjoyed him and many of whom were truly fond of him, he was with a girl.

Didi kept his groups of friends separate, only rarely carrying a girl from one group across the frontiers of another. At first I used to think this was because he felt they would have little in common – they were a diverse lot – and later I had moments of cynicism when I thought that since he had no money and had to batten to some extent on whoever he was with, it was so that he could move away to fresh pastures when hospitality began to wear thin. Now I believe it was more complex than that. Some of the friends he had made in the past had to be kept apart because he had given them different and conflicting 'versions' of himself, but chiefly he was instinctively protecting himself against his own fickleness. After a period, sometimes several months, of being very intimate with one lot of friends, seeing them every day, enjoying them with open-hearted affection, he would 'go off' them. Suddenly they would become insufferably tedious to him and he would start telling me that they were 'stupid', 'superficial', 'terrible bores'. But he knew they hadn't changed and that it was only his 'insanity' at work. He would move away from that lot of friends – sometimes cut himself off from them completely to the point of telling them that he had gone abroad – and plunge into an equally close intimacy with another lot; and after a few weeks or months the irritation would pass and he would again be able to meet the first lot with enjoyment. The fickleness was something he was unable to overcome, but it was on the surface. Fundamentally Didi went on loving anyone of whom he was really fond, and would always go back to them with affection and appreciation after the necessary 'rest'.

He brought home funny or interesting stories from all this social activity, and sometimes, if they were 'special', he brought home girls. When he had finished the work resulting from the Six Day War he took on the editing of a manuscript, and talked a good deal about it. Although he clearly wasn't doing the work he talked about – he was doing nothing but stay in bed until opening time, come back for a siesta when the pubs closed, get up to go out again at about seven o'clock, and return to bed at three or four or five in the morning – I didn't fret about him. I had stopped hoping that he would ever work except under the influence of some extraordinary stimulus. So long as he was not in a depressive crisis, so long as he appeared to be getting pleasure out of his life and was therefore able to be agreeable, he was – I had come to feel – 'all right'. By now I had stopped worrying about him – or rather, had started avoiding it by comic resignation to the future existence of my old man in carpet slippers.

It was this resignation which blinded me to what was really going on. The truth was that in accepting that I would have Didi with me for ever I had given him up. I was no longer focusing on him, no longer really caring much about him. It had stopped being painful to have him about the place, and it was no longer, as it had been to start with, delightful. Sometimes it was amusing or pleasant, at other times it was mildly annoying – he broke a lot of my china, for instance, and had always taken the screwdriver when I happened to need it – but it had stopped being *interesting*. I had other preoccupations now. He had to have a home somewhere so all right, he could have one under my roof, but I had run out of other things to give him, and anyway he asked for nothing else. At least, I told myself, there hadn't been another distinct crisis since 'Crisis Diana'; a year went by – more than a year – without one, and that hadn't happened for a long time; so perhaps the security he now had, although it was obviously not going to change him much, was of some help to him after all.

Didi knew that I had given him up, but while the fact was a relief to me, to him it was something different.

How my life will continue from here it is impossible to visualize. There is no prospect of any money coming in to me at all. Diana, I instinctively know, has given up. Given up in the sense that knowing she is too kind – that it would be against her innermost nature – to put me out of the door, she is resigned to leaving me alone and to paying the expenses which, as I have said before, sap her of all items of luxury which she is entitled to through her work and writing-earnings. Not only is she resigned to my presence – she makes it as agreeable as possible for both of us. She is charming to me – and my heart bleeds for her.

There was hardly a day during this period when Didi seemed so gay and carefree that he didn't wake up to the knowledge that he was soon going to kill himself. It was worse than 'being in a dep'. It was because what he recognized as the symptoms of 'a dep' were absent that it was so bad. Lacking those symptoms, he didn't look at himself and say 'I am ill'; he looked at himself and said 'I am hopeless'.

He was approaching forty. He was not earning his living. He knew that however much he argued with himself he was never going to earn his living. He was going to continue living as a parasite on his friends, even when he could see clearly that they couldn't afford it. He was costing me – he worked it out carefully – not only the £5 a week I would otherwise be getting for his room, but also his heating, his telephoning, much of his eating, and he knew that it was now two years since I'd earned any extra money by writing and that I was falling into debt. He didn't pretend not to know this. He wrote it down – and when he finally 'solved' the problem it was not in a way which could alleviate guilt because he did it by accepting money from another woman – a friend of rare generosity and kindness – with which to pay me. And he was costing many of his other friends money too: sometimes the odd few pounds, sometimes quite large sums. He kept a record. And when he took this money, what did he do with it? He drank it or gambled it, and he wrote that down too. While as for the most important thing in his life – love – there he was either a brute or a child: the one thing he could be sure of concerning his loves was that he would wreck them. It was true that he would be the chief sufferer from this, but the suffering was no expiation because it was of his own making. He was without hope.

During all of the last fifteen months of his life Didi was simply skating desperately over thin ice. Almost every morning there would be an ominous whine as a crack snaked over its surface, and swiftly he would skate away from that patch. A new girl to make; an evening's drunken gaiety; an illusion of love; a Saturday afternoon when he could scoot from pub to betting shop, trying for a treble; an amusing new acquaintance who responded to his charm; an occasional mellow evening with Luke and me, talking about writing ... he would dart from one to another of these *reasons for not dying just yet*, and I believed him to be 'all right'.

I suspect now that it was the very security he had gained in finding a home, and someone he could trust not to throw him out, which finally made the ice give way. He had supposed that given this chance he would change, and he hadn't changed, which brought his reason in as a dangerous ally to his unreason. Because the unreasonable sense of insecurity was still as strong as ever.

A few months before his death he had made me angry. I was having a room painted and asked Didi either to be in the flat at midday to let the painter in, or to leave his key in the door. He did neither, causing both the painter and myself a good deal of inconvenience, and instead of apologizing he protested aggressively that the painter had been rude to him about it. 'If that bastard speaks to me like that again I'll punch his face,' he screamed, and I, losing my temper, said 'If you do that you know what you can ...' and then bit it off and left the room. This is what he wrote about the incident.

The situation I am in now has been typical since boyhood. No one putting up with me. Whatever unorthodox or mischievous thing I did met with 'He must go away'. Where to? From Grandpa's to Tante B, to my mother, to the S's, to the J's, to Dolly for a couple of nights, from Alex to Cairo to Alex to Cairo to Alex. Each autumn, the end of summer, I would be staying with friends – school would be starting again soon and I had to go 'back'. But 'back' where? To whom? The Cairo school or the Alex school? I would stand, my heart sinking inside me, with my suitcases, in the street as it were. Dolly would finally 'arrange' something (never at her place, though). Finally a *pension*, when I was still a boy, and never any home since. I keep thinking about all that. And this, I suppose, turns you into a manic-depressive, presumably incapable of 'coping with life'. What shall I do?

When to the panic of this frightened child there was added an adult's awareness of his own 'impossibility', what indeed could he do?

I had naively hoped that if he could be made to feel that someone's affection would endure whatever he did, his sense of his own value might be restored, but it worked the other way. The kinder and more patient people were with him, the more evil he felt himself to be. If I had ever accused him of costing me more than I could afford he would have been able to despise my meanness or otherwise work up some rationalization for what he was doing. Because I was silent he had to accuse himself. He didn't believe that I went on loving him because he was lovable. He believed that I went on being kind to him because I was good, and what help was that? He was partly right, too. Strands of various kinds of love there certainly were in what I felt for him, but by now the bulk of my motive in accepting him as a responsibility came from a conception of how I would act if I were good, and my having got used to behaving in that way – and that, I suppose, is what most 'goodness' is: not, as it turned out, a way of behaving of any value in a situation like this one.

Something else which I had supposed might be helpful proved instead to be the opposite. I had believed that the more a sick person knew about himself, the more likely he would be to find means of dealing with his sickness, but to stay alive Didi needed illusion, not truth. He needed to be persuaded that he was other than he was by seeing reflected back at him from other people an image which he could accept. He was adept – extraordinarily adept – at bringing this about if he could avoid being too close to people for too long, which was why he was most at his ease in pubs and at parties and in the first stages of capturing a girl: situations in which he could almost infallibly be seen as the kind of man he ought to be. But now he was living all the time with someone who knew him too well, and whom he knew too well. I never taxed him with his short-comings because I knew before he came to stay with me how precarious his balance was; but he knew how I felt behind my silence about his drinking, his gambling, his attitude to women, his self-deceptions. When we talked about them, as we some-times did, it was because *he* liked – or thought he liked – being able at times to discuss himself with someone who wasn't fooled, but who nevertheless accepted and forgave him.

'I've started having to be very drunk, now, before I can make love to her.'

'Oh darling – wouldn't it be better to leave her alone?'

'Much better, but you know me.'

'How long is it since you've been able to make love to anyone sober?'

'Not for years – years and years.'

'It's bad, love, isn't it?'

'Yes, it's very bad.'

While such a conversation was going on, Didi felt that it was relaxing and comforting, but in fact it amounted to a confron-tation. He looked into the mirror of another person – and he saw himself as he was.

And during this period two things happened, one minor and one genuinely tragic, which affected Didi deeply.

The first was the loss of his car. Belatedly and courteously the police caught up with him and told him that he must regis-ter it in this country, before which it would have to pass a test, and it would have needed a great deal of money spent on it before it could do that. Battered, crumpled, scraped, one-eyed, it was the most disreputable Volkswagen in London. Didi loved it too much to have it scrapped – and even I agreed that it was hard not to attribute gallantry to that dilapidated little machine, which continued to run so impeccably and to consume so little oil and petrol in defiance of its own condition – so instead he 'laid it up' in an adventure playground run by a friend of his. He knew well enough that the children would have it stripped to the chassis within a week, but to speak of 'laying up' was less cruel than to speak of 'scrapping'.

In losing his car Didi was losing far more than a convenient means of getting about. His last symbol of 'style' had gone, his last prop in his act of being independent. He knew, of course, that it was outrageous that someone without a penny should run a car at all, however frugal, and he had the grace to accept its loss with outward cheerfulness; but he felt as though he were amputated, not only of a means of locomotion, but of a facet of his personality which was truly important to him.

The other event was the death of his friend Peter in Düsseldorf, from some form of cancer. Didi had seen Peter only twice since he had left Germany, but he was constantly aware of his presence in life as someone he truly loved and admired, and his grief at Peter's death was overwhelming. It was simple and complete – the kind of emotion he prided himself on, in genuine operation. His incredulous misery at the fact that Peter was gone was so great that I doubt whether he was able to perceive one of its consequences to himself, although that consequence existed. While Peter was alive, Didi still had an escape hatch. He hadn't the least desire to return to Germany, but if for some reason his condition in London became intolerable, then Peter-in-Düsseldorf was there to play the part which Diana-in-London had played when Germany became intolerable: he could provide an alternative to suicide. Whether Didi ever formulated this thought to himself I do not know, but I am sure that Peter's death left a wound deeper than the great one he acknowledged.

In spite of increased detachment, as the Christmas of 1968 approached I noticed signs that there was a bad time ahead. Didi had started to suffer from insomnia – a danger signal far graver than I understood – and was depending more and more on sleeping pills, which he procured in twos and threes from a friend too sensible to hand them over in any quantity. I could also see that he was stepping up his drinking again, although he disguised from me the fact that he had started to 'borrow' more recklessly than ever and to cash dud cheques in order to gamble.

Another ill omen was that he began to destroy his current love affair, one which had lasted longer than usual and was far better grounded than most of them, on which I had started to pin hopes (not of anything so unlikely as marriage, but of an improvement in his ability to 'see' a woman). This girl he liked and enjoyed as a person. It was true that he was unable to summon up any very strong sexual passion for her – that was something he could never do with any woman to whom he was drawn by affection and esteem instead of by the flash of illusion – but he had said of her 'For the first time I've started to see what you and Luke mean when you say that truly liking someone is the most important thing in love. I do truly like her, and it's marvellous.' I had been very pleased about this. I was charmed by the girl, recognizing over the gulf of years between us a woman with whom I would enjoy friendship, and I had been seeing his relationship with her, together with the longer than usual absence of a full-scale depressive crisis, as an encouraging sign. A little before Christmas, however, I began to notice symptoms which I recognized only too clearly, and I knew that the girl would soon have to leave him in self-defence and that the crisis into which he would then plunge would be serious.

I was, however, far from realizing how bad things already were. Here is his diary entry for December 18, the last before that of December 26.

About ten days ago – the day after the last entry, in fact – I once again did what I have often done in my life: got drunk and went berserk and spent some days in my although-indescribable yet often-described-here mess. Even as I write I know it will not be the last time, and that it will probably happen over and over again. Gambling seems to be replacing sex with me. The same thrill, heart-beat, exuberance I used to feel at an anticipated conquest I now feel prior to gambling and, like sex, I want it more – and I am more daring when drunk.

Last Wednesday Anne [the friend who gave him money to pay my rent] asked me to supper. We had a few drinks, then someone phoned her for a party and of course I told her to go. She had also asked a young pseudo-actress (hopeless type) to come to supper, so I said I'd take care of the girl. Anne gave me $100 to pay the rent for two months and spend the rest. The girl came, very pretty, very young, with hair falling down to her waist. We drank, got drunk, ate, danced, flirted. I had borrowed P's car for the evening. The girl and I drove back here for 'coffee'. I drank whisky and suddenly got the gambling bug. Dressed, took the girl, and drunkenly drove to the club. Lost the $100. Returned home at about 4 a.m. with the girl. We slept but I didn't touch her. She woke me at 8, I drove her to the station, wrote a letter to P (I was still very drunk) to say I was desperate, enclosed a cheque and asked her to lend me money. I took her the letter, the car and the cheque and came home to sleep. Thursday was a terrible day. Margaret [the girl he was having an affair with] came in the morning and I told her what I had done. Then L phoned up – P had already told him. He said, bless him, to go to his place at once. I called a taxi, went to a pub with Margaret, cashed an impossible cheque for £5, drank more whisky, lost another £2 on the horses, then together with Margaret went to L's. Drank a bottle of wine, ate something, went upstairs with L – and burst into tears. Oh lord oh lord oh lord. An orgy of despising myself. P said she would lend me some money. Calmed down, drank some more, then came home with Margaret. Poor Margaret. Next morning, physically, mentally and financially bankrupt, I went to P's parents to cook for them. One look at P and I knew she was taking back yesterday's promise. She drove me mad – mad with her 'advice'. It killed me, and I still don't know whether she is simple-minded or simply a hypocrite. 'Tell your bank manager,' she says, 'they *like* helping foreigners' – 'tell him', she says, 'that you'll cook for my parents now and then and get paid for it – tell him you'll be baby-sitting ... '

'Yes,' I told her, 'I shall.' I loathed her at that moment. She's worth about a quarter of a million ON HER OWN.

She left, and I took her mother's car to do the shopping. The house overlooks the park. Overlooks? It's IN the bloody park and is littered with Picasso, Utrillo, Chagall, Kokoshka, one Matisse, one Degas, one Renoir ... and when I tell her mother that I need some whisky for cooking (to drink, of course) she goes and opens a bar and comes back with a bottle of Martell.

'Is this whisky?' she asks.

'No,' I say.

Half feverishly, miserably, hating myself, I spend six hours in their kitchen and cook them food they never even knew existed.

'What's that?'

'Courgettes.'

'And that?'

'CELERY.'

'Oh.'

Gave me 70s for my work and I walked home wondering whether really it isn't time I effaced myself. Nothing but a sponger, a liar, hypocrite, weak-minded spoilt idiot. Friday I had a bath, pinched some sleeping pills from downstairs and slept well – to awake rather refreshed, blast me. Saturday I quarrelled with Margaret. She, no wonder, was slightly patronizing and – no wonder – despising. Told her to bugger off and leave me alone. This was my life and if she didn't like it she could lump it.

'But my life is involved with yours,' she pleaded.

'Well I'm not going to be converted into a dowdy, middle-class mediocrity' I shouted back – oh unfair, unfair – again blast me.

Sunday I wouldn't see her. Monday I phoned up B and told that woman I'm editing for I was in a mess and she said she'd pay for the work I'm doing for her (more of that later) – gave me a cheque for £20. That night I went to B's office, and he gave me a cheque for £110.

There is no moral in the story, of course. Never has been. I pick myself up, work for three or four days, arrange things slightly and I don't even despise myself any more. The only morality which is correct, as far as I am concerned, is that it would be immoral to take all this from my friends and be miserable at the same time. That would be terribly immoral.

Margaret said she'd part from me and I agreed it was

right. I really am too fond of her to want to see her life bug-
gered. So she did leave me for two days, but came back
again.

And last Saturday I bought ... a car! Oh dear oh dear oh
dear. Yes, a car. Reg gave it to me for £10. Nice little Ford,
so there. Sunday was invited to a party, but although there
were some nice people there I was bored, so DROVE back
early to bed. Have been working quite hard on the editing –
mustn't fail to describe that woman tomorrow. *Et voilà* –

Didi drove me to the station in his new car on Christmas Eve. I
had left a note for him in the hall the night before – he was out
late, as usual – saying 'Will you be able to drive me to the
station? Just scribble "yes" or "no" and leave this out for me.'
He didn't leave the note out, but emerged from his room next
morning to say that of course he would do it. Later I was to find
the note on his desk with a great drunken 'NO' scrawled on it –
he must have woken early, or been unable to sleep, and
retrieved it before I got up.

He looked exhausted and complained of the number of
parties he had been asked to during the Christmas holiday. 'It's
this bloody not-sleeping,' he said. I said why not take one day
off from parties, anyway, and have a restful domestic time at
home. 'Yes, I think I will do that,' he said – and perhaps he did.
There were six pairs of socks drying – or rather, thoroughly
dry – in the bathroom when I got back. He carried my suitcase
into the train for me and put it on the rack, and we said goodbye
in the compartment. He gave me a kiss and a smile so loving
that I thought 'Bless him, he *is* still my old Didi and not just a
bore, in spite of everything.'

Didi went to two of the parties and impressed the people he was
with as being cheerful in a relaxed way and as drinking less than
usual. The evening of Boxing Day, however, was different.
Where he went I do not know, but what is certain is that he got
very drunk, went to a gambling club and lost everything that
was left of his recently 'borrowed' money. He came home with
a friend – people downstairs heard them talking and laughing

– and a bottle of whisky. When his friend had gone he went downstairs to my cousin's flat and crept into her kitchen, where she keeps her medicine chest. He knew that she used sleeping pills on prescription and sometimes sneaked one or two when his own strictly limited supply was inadequate. This time he took the whole bottle.

This is the last entry in his diary, five volumes of which he left stacked neatly on a kitchen stool in my bedroom:

> I am going to kill myself tonight. The beginning of this diary said 'I must write this record as I am going to kill myself' [It didn't]. The time has come. I am, of course, drunk. But then sober it would have been very very very difficult (– I acknowledge the drunken writing myself). But what else could I do, sweethearts? loved ones? Nothing, really. Nothing. Diana sweetheart, I cannot apologize because that would be just too hypocritical. Of course I should not have left this scene behind. But I am lazy, I am spoilt. I am leaving you my diary, luv. Well-edited, it could be a good piece of literature. If it is, the following are my debts.

He then listed all his major debts; going back five years.

> It all amounts to less than £1000 – what I owe you I don't even mention. Whatever I have – post-earn – is yours with the hope that you will first if possible pay those above debts.
>
> It had to happen, sweetheart. My life is simply a matter of postponing – putting it off, off, and really at last it was time, and rather convenient at this time.
>
> Diana, to you I do not have to write very much. You understood, and of course realized that I had to end up like this. I leave you my last four–five years' diary (my life) – which, obviously, you understand I would leave to the person I love most – you.
>
> Sweetheart Margaret, there are *actual real* tragedies in life and the obvious tragedy is that of despair. I have lied, sponged, been hypocritical, dished out impossible cheques – but I have also, in spite of all that, sometimes been terribly

honest and even very sincere. All my books, my fluffy gorilla [a toy-mascot he kept in his room] belong to you – and I am sure Diana will give them to you (except for some books which actually belong to Diana).

And the most dramatic moment of my life – the only authentic one – is a terrible let-down. – I have already swallowed my death. I could vomit it out if I wanted to. Honestly and sincerely, I really don't want to. It is a pleasure. I am doing this not in a sad, unhappy way; but on the contrary, happily and even (a state of being and a word I have always loved) SERENELY … serenely.

He added an almost illegible four-line postscript about what to do with his car, then he must have taken the diary into my room, and written the note the police found pinned to the door of his own: 'DIANA, DON'T COME IN. PHONE 999.'

Because he made that telephone call to a friend – made it, I guess, after he had written the words 'a terrible let-down', where a break occurs – he was found and taken to hospital within an hour. They pumped him out. I was telephoned, but was snowed in with twelve miles of impassable country lanes between me and the railway station, which I couldn't reach for three days. It didn't matter, they said, he was still unconscious and unable to recognize anyone – even if he survived it would be days before he fully recovered consciousness. The hospital would say little, but Margaret, who was with him all the time, gave full and honest reports. The chances of his living were small, but they existed.

They were strange, grey days, those days before I was able to get back to London. There was little *shock* in them. Once I had imagined him shooting himself in front of me as his cousin had done in front of his mother, and myself thinking coldly 'Poor little bastard, now he's done it', and when I got the first telephone call it wasn't so very different, only softer: 'My poor little love, he's done it at last.' I hadn't been expecting him to do it *now* – not this time – not yet … but he was right, of course. It had been an optimistic joke, the image of my old man in carpet slippers. No other end was imaginable for him, and I had known it. Chiefly, during those days before I could get back to London, I concentrated on the possibility of his recovery, plans for getting him to a psychiatrist (he couldn't dodge it now), efforts to brace myself to the fact that if he lived the future couldn't be anything but difficult and exhausting. I saw that it could be managed. It would be a matter of doing what had to be done, first one thing, then the next thing, as they came up – that, I saw, is how people get through situations much worse than this one, such as having their husbands felled by a stroke, or their children crippled. They don't, when it comes to it, expend their energy on plumbing the horror of their situation, they simply do what has to be done.

When at last I got to the hospital there was hope in the air. Margaret greeted me with the news that he was better. At first, she said, they'd had to strap him down because his body was thrashing and heaving, and he was howling all the time, but now he was quiet, and for the first time he was recognizing people.

I think he was, too. When someone bent over him and touched him, his eyes, after swimming about, would gradually fix on the face above him, and slowly expression would dawn in them: a sweet smile, followed by a look of distress, sometimes by tears. He seemed to recognize me, and I like to imagine that when the expression of distress gave way to one of peace while I was very softly stroking his hand and murmuring to him, he knew that I was there. (Later, on that same visit, when I touched him again, he pushed my hand away as though it were hurting him, twisting and turning on his pillow.)

But that was his last 'good' day. Two days later examination by a specialist revealed great and increasing damage to his brain, and we knew that even if he survived physically his mind was lost.

They said he was deeply unconscious. How can they be sure? If a body moans endlessly for ten days, twisting itself this way and that, it must still be exchanging messages of some sort with the brain. It is true that a hand or a light could be passed before his eyes without their reacting, and he didn't know whether people were there or not, speaking to him or touching him or not; but his body still protested pitifully when they did painful things to it such as inserting up his nostril the tube through which he was drip-fed. Perhaps it was only the dimmest dream of pain which still existed in his skull, but watching him I was unable to be convinced that there was nothing there. On the Sunday morning when the ward-sister telephoned to say that he was gone, the whole house, the trees and grass outside my window, seemed suddenly to go still with relief. They may have been right. He may have been 'gone' long before he died. But what had been lying in that bed had seemed to me to be Didi in profound agony.

I am not often able to grieve fully. The watcher is usually there, noting what is inadequate or incongruous, observing the unexpected, wondering at the odd. For Didi I grieved fully, though not when I most appeared to be doing so. That must have been when they were lowering him into his grave, and I wept. But my tears surprised me. It had been going on for so long – the ten days of his dying, and then another fifteen for the autopsy, the inquest and lining up for a place in a cemetery – that I thought all feeling must be exhausted and that the funeral itself would be meaningless. When I found myself unable to move forward to the edge of the grave, the tears running down my face and the sobs mounting so that I had to clench my teeth or I would have howled, it was something which was happening to me rather than something I was doing.

The grieving came before that, not as an emotional convulsion but as a long stare at the intolerable after I had read the diary he left me from beginning to end. It was not intolerable that he had killed himself. It was intolerable that he had been right to do so – that he had no alternative. It was intolerable that a man should be so crippled by things done to him in his defenceless childhood that he had been made, literally and precisely, unendurable to himself. He had tried to change. All through his adult life the part of him which he thought of as his 'mental sanity' had stood in the wings and watched the part he called 'emotional insanity' – watched and judged, in vain. His intelligence, his gifts – useless to him. Other people's patience, kindness, affection, understanding – useless to him. Love? Too late, and equally useless. I for one could have loved Didi more and better than I did, but all that would have happened then would have been that he'd have had more love to disbelieve in. He was certain at too deep a level, in the very fibres of his being, that he was unworthy of love. Being unworthy of love, he must be punished; and the only way he could secure this was by plunging out to the point where he was driven to punish himself. To be murdered would be a fate much simpler, and less sad.

This record has been written for him, and for people who are going to have children.

For further information about Granta Books
and a full list of titles, please write to us at

Granta Books

2/3 HANOVER YARD

NOEL ROAD

LONDON

N1 8BE

enclosing a stamped, addressed envelope

_____

You can visit our website at

http://www.granta.com